T0301002

# ROUTLEDGE LIBRARY EDITIONS: ALCOHOL AND ALCOHOLISM

Volume 3

# ALCOHOLIC BEVERAGES

# ALCOHOLIC BEVERAGES

## JOHN CAVANAGH
### AND
## FREDERICK F. CLAIRMONTE

Routledge
Taylor & Francis Group

LONDON AND NEW YORK

First published in 1985 by Croom Helm Ltd

This edition first published in 2024
by Routledge
4 Park Square, Milton Park, Abingdon, Oxon OX14 4RN

and by Routledge
605 Third Avenue, New York, NY 10158

*Routledge is an imprint of the Taylor & Francis Group, an informa business*

*British Library Cataloguing in Publication Data*
A catalogue record for this book is available from the British Library

ISBN: 978-1-032-59082-0 (Set)
ISBN: 978-1-032-60376-6 (Volume 3) (hbk)
ISBN: 978-1-032-60538-8 (Volume 3) (pbk)
ISBN: 978-1-003-45888-3 (Volume 3) (ebk)

DOI: 10.4324/9781003458883

**Publisher's Note**
The publisher has gone to great lengths to ensure the quality of this reprint but points out that some imperfections in the original copies may be apparent.

**Disclaimer**
The publisher has made every effort to trace copyright holders and would welcome correspondence from those they have been unable to trace.

# ALCOHOLIC BEVERAGES

## DIMENSIONS OF CORPORATE POWER

John Cavanagh and Frederick F. Clairmonte

CROOM HELM
London & Sydney

©1985 John Cavanagh and Frederick F. Clairmonte
Croom Helm Ltd, Provident House, Burrell Row,
Beckenham, Kent BR3 1AT
Croom Helm Australia Pty Ltd, First Floor, 139 King Street,
Sydney, NSW 2001, Australia

British Library Cataloguing in Publication Data
Cavanagh, John
  Alcoholic beverages: dimensions of
  corporate power.
  1. Alcoholic beverage industry
  I. Title   II. Clairmonte, Frederick F.
  338.4'76631    HD3950.5

ISBN 0-7099-3439-4

Printed and Bound in Great Britain

# CONTENTS

## LIST OF TABLES

# LIST OF FIGURES

# LIST OF ABBREVIATIONS

| | |
|---|---|
| BAT | British American Tobacco |
| CUB | Carlton and United Breweries |
| CPE | Centrally Planned Economies |
| DCL | Distillers Company Ltd |
| DE | Developing Economies |
| DME | Developed Market Economies |
| EEC | European Economic Community |
| FAO | Food and Agriculture Organization |
| FTC | Federal Trade Commission |
| ICI | Imperial Chemical Industries |
| IDV | International Distillers and Vintners |
| NDCC | National Distillers and Chemical Corporation |
| NEDC | National Economic Development Council |
| SAB | South African Breweries |
| TNB | Transnational Bank |
| TNC | Transnational Corporation |
| UNCTAD | United Nations Conference on Trade and Development |
| USDA | US Department of Agriculture |
| WHO | World Health Organization |

# ACKNOWLEDGEMENTS

Such an enterprise would have been inconceivable without generous assistance and unwavering support of many individuals.

Among former and current World Health Organization officials, we extend special thanks to Monique Cahannes, Elfriede Duane, Marcus Grant, Jacques Hamon, Jan Ording and Nedd Willard.

World Health Organization advisers who provided timely advice and assistance on earlier drafts include: Virginia Beardshaw, Sally Casswell, John Ebie, David Hawks, Pat Morgan, Torbjorn Mork, Jim Mosher, Robin Room, Irv Rootman, Haydee Rosovsky, Namposya Serpell, Eric Single, Pekka Sulkunen, Lee Towle and Bo Wickstrom.

Others whose input and support was extremely helpful include: Annelies Allain, Robin Broad, Anwar Fazal, Martin Khor, Judy Mann, Diego Ozarnum, Ted Wheelwright, the statistical staff of the Addiction Research Centre in Canada, the staff of the International Trade Centre library, the staff of the UK Brewers Society, and the statistical staff of the UNCTAD secretariat.

In corporate research of this nature, there are always many who offer support but whose position demands anonymity. They know who they are, and we remain grateful that they continue to supply information despite the many risks involved.

With thankful acknowledgement of all the assistance, the ideas expressed in this book remain those of the authors alone. We welcome the debate that their publication will engender.

John Cavanagh
Washington, D.C.

Frederick Clairmonte
Geneva, Switzerland

# PREFACE

To speak and write of alcohol problems without reference to the burgeoning transnational corporations that produce and market alcoholic beverages is akin to a discourse on *Hamlet* without reference to the Prince. Yet, this is precisely what certain institutions and individuals have done for decades and continue to do to this day.

This book, researched over a period of several years, was preceded by the authors' extensive work within the United Nations Conference on Trade and Development (UNCTAD) on the impact of transnational corporations on global markets. These previous studies attempted to illuminate how the tempo of corporate expansion has made gigantic strides in all economic sectors and shows no signs of letting up. The metamorphosis of corporate power is witnessed in the soaring revenues of the world's top two hundred industrial corporations. Merely over the last two decades, their share of the world's gross national product rocketed from 17 to 29 per cent. Conversely, by the end of the current decade, tens of thousands of medium- and small-scale enterprises will have been liquidated, many of them in the alcohol sector.

In the course of our researches, past and present, we have been struck by the extent to which global corporations, with their imbricated production, financial and marketing structures, continue to remain shadowy, evasive and largely unknown. Their highly touted, but singularly uninformative, annual reports convenient serve to obfuscate the ramifications of their mounting global operations.

Public non-accountability pervades the practices of these firms, in that their corporate decisions, notwithstanding their vociferous claims to the contrary, remain unanswerable to those directly or indirectly affected by their policies. The mammoth alcohol corporations, thanks to their masterly public relations exercises and influence on the media, have cast a spell on all forms of enquiry geared to illuminate their operational workings, strikingly so in their impact on the health of tens of millions in both the developed and developing countries.

The overriding goal of this enquiry has been to collect and systematise a vast array of chaotic fact heaps, scrap piles of corporate documentation and oral evidence, and beat them into the first comprehensive attempt at conceptualising the grip of corporate power over this sector. The authors are under no illusion that they have exhaustively explored all the intricacies of the web of corporate accountability and non-accountability in the alcohol sector. Rather, their aim has been to demystify the extent to which corporate alcohol power has obscured the economic and political forces in which it is enmeshed and of which it has been the beneficiary.

In short, the authors have attempted to come to grips with the essence, as distinct from the appearances so characteristic of formal discussions in certain international fora, of the corporate forces that are inseparable from the production, marketing and control of alcoholic beverages.

# INTRODUCTION:
# CORPORATE POWER AND PUBLIC HEALTH

Public health is inseparable from the political, economic and social framework in which people live, work and die.[1] The central focus of this book is corporate power as it influences a specific range of addictive commodities — alcoholic beverages — whose output, marketing and distribution are increasingly dominated by large-scale Transnational Corporations (TNCs).[2] Problems generated by alcohol consumption[3] cannot be grasped without far-reaching analyses of this roughly $170 billion global alcohol market — a figure which demarcates the boundaries of this study.[4]

## Corporate Power and Consumption

Previous studies have demonstrated that a relationship exists between increased alcoholic beverage consumption and a rise in its harmful consequences.[5] This book explores for the first time another crucial relationship, namely the link between corporate structures and the availability and consumption of alcoholic beverages.[6]

For most of the post-war period, alcohol problems have been viewed primarily as individual problems. More recently, the investigatory approach of many researchers has highlighted the importance of larger socio-economic factors in shaping drinking levels, patterns and problems.[7] While this approach represents a distinctive step forward in understanding alcohol-related problems, it has largely ignored a paramount force that conditions this larger socio-economic environment: the modern TNC.

## Consequences of Concentration

At the onset of the twentieth century, alcoholic beverage output, as with many other industries, was largely under the control of small firms whose distributional reach was local and, in limited cases, regional. Over the ensuing decades, this industrial structure was to

1

undergo a dramatic metamorphosis through accelerated capital accumulation within alcoholic beverage firms, characterised by waves of mergers and acquisitions. This paved the way for large corporate units which vastly extended their output and distribution networks nationally.[8] This concentration was most conspicuous in the beer and distilled spirits sectors, where already by the mid-1960s a handful of giant corporations had achieved market dominance in most countries. In this drive to oligopoly,[9] most wine sectors lagged behind. In many countries, concentration led to a prodigious increase in the availability and diversity of commercial alcoholic beverages that penetrated even the remotest rural areas.

Concentration in output was paralleled by concentration in retailing, albeit at a slower pace. Most significant for alcohol sales has been the striking growth of multiple retail chains in several Developed Market Economies (DMEs), increasingly marketing their own alcoholic beverage brands. This has contributed to augment alcoholic beverage availability, usually at lower retail prices.

What, it may be asked in the global context of public health, were the constellation of forces that propelled alcoholic beverages beyond national frontiers? Under the impetus of the post-Second World War economic boom and the concomitant upsurge in incomes, consumption of alcoholic beverages in many DMEs grew rapidly over the 1950s and 1960s. With the economic slowdown of the 1970s, however, there were signs of decelerating consumption in many of these markets, compelling the larger corporate producers to seek markets elsewhere. This economic movement coincided with rapid technological strides in transportation and telecommunications, which facilitated the globalisation of marketing and managerial decision-making.

Just as the preceding developments could be considered as factors pushing alcohol on global markets, there were parallel developments that contributed to pull alcohol towards countries where consumption was traditionally low. Paramount among these pull factors in post-independence Developing Economies (DEs) was the unprecedented migration from non-monetised rural areas to monetised urban aggregations. This was accompanied in many DEs by a vast numerical increase in elites with high purchasing power and westernised consumption patterns. Related to these changes in several newly independent countries was the implementation of import substitution industrialisation policies, which spurred the setting up of domestic breweries.

This global configuration of push and pull factors catalysed big firms in the beer and distilled spirits sectors to extend their operations overseas into both DEs and DMEs. Among the pioneers in the transnationalisation of the beer sector were the quasi-monopolies Heineken (Netherlands), United Breweries (Denmark), and Guinness (UK/Ireland), each controlling over three-fifths of their national markets by the 1960s.[10] Overseas penetration by distilled spirit firms was spearheaded by the highly oligopolistic whisky sectors in the UK and North America, and the giant cognac houses of France.[11] More recently, the increasingly concentrated champagne sector in France and wine sector in a few other countries have also extended operations considerably on global markets.

These overseas salients were made via three corporate mechanisms: exports of goods,[12] exports of capital[13] and sales of licenses.[14] The combined impact of these three has influenced the availability, variety and consumption of alcoholic beverages in DMEs and DEs. Out of 46 countries where beer output grew more than 50 per cent between 1975 and 1980, 42 were DEs, with the overwhelming bulk of output consumed nationally. Indicative of the consequences of distilled spirits expansion was that, by 1977, 36 DEs depended on imports from TNCs for over a fifth of their distilled spirits consumption.[15]

Penetration of the global market is but one mechanism whereby concentrated corporate power influences consumption. Yet another is that sectoral control by an exiguous number of firms can, at times, engender collusive business practices. Such behavioural patterns are not the sole preserve of oligopolies comprised of TNCs, but are also seen in markets controlled by a handful of powerful domestic entrepreneurs.[16] Market-sharing arrangements and other such collaborative practices enhance each corporation's promotional and distributional power to mould consumer behaviour.

## Impact of Conglomeration[17]

Concomitant with the dramatic rise in corporate concentration over the last two decades has been a related phenomenon which has exercised a no less deleterious impact on health: the growth of the globe-girdling conglomerate. In the quest for profitable investment outlets, TNCs have increasingly annexed firms in unrelated fields of business.

Historically, an initial phase in conglomeration is often marked by corporate overspill into more than one alcoholic beverage sector, most notably distilled spirits companies entering the wine sector. In different countries, various combinations of such straddling operations can be seen, often involving extensions into soft drinks and other beverages. One of the important policy implications of this conglomerate movement is that it confers on these diverse sectors a unity which can be translated into enormous political leverage.

A second and no less important phase is an expansionary drive beyond the borders of alcohol. Of the 27 alcoholic-beverage-producing TNCs which recorded sales of over $1 billion (1980), almost all had extensive output and marketing operations outside the realm of alcohol. Noteworthy is that these comprise such massive producers of alcoholic beverages as R. J. Reynolds (through its subsidiary Heublein), Coca Cola (through its subsidiary Wine Spectrum) and Lonrho (through its subsidiary John Holt), whose alcohol sales nonetheless represent but a minor share of their total operations.

Such conglomerate extensions, often substantially underpinned by large Transnational Banks (TNBs), bear directly on consumption and health via two mechanisms. In the first place, they create the conditions for widespread deployment of cross subsidisation, whereby a firm can shift gains from profitable segments of its operations to subsidise losses in others. A pioneer in the adaptation of this technique for alcohol expansion was Philip Morris, which bought a minor regional US brewer (Miller) in 1969, and propelled it into the world's second biggest brewer by 1980. Funnelling profits from another addictive product line — tobacco — it underpriced competitors in new markets and thus contributed to stimulate the overall level of beer consumption.

Secondly, conglomerate acquisitions of alcoholic beverage corporations in many cases are by TNCs with extensive international networks for other consumer products. Alcohol, therefore, becomes merely one more commodity adapted to a shared distribution network, thereby effectively reaching more consumers. Nowhere has the impact of conglomeration on alcohol consumption been so conspicuous as in the extensive link-ups between five transnational tobacco conglomerates[18] that have dominated world cigarette markets and alcohol corporations: Philip Morris and Miller; R. J. Reynolds and Heublein; the Imperial Group and Courage; American Brands and Jim Beam; and the Rembrandt/Rothmans Group and its extensive wine interests.

As producers and purveyors of one addictive commodity, tobacco, they have brought well-tested expertise culled over many decades to the marketing of another, alcohol. Among the highly successful techniques that have been adapted to further their conquests of national and international alcohol markets are market segmentation, brand differentiation and sporting events sponsorship. These techniques are having an increasing impact on developing countries, as tobacco TNCs counter a slowdown of cigarette consumption in DMEs by enlarging their market salients in developing countries. The self-reinforcing corporate linkages between these two addictive commodities on the global market become even more pronounced in the perspective of health, as evidence surfaces that the combination of alcohol and tobacco consumption further enhances the incidence of harmful effects.

## Marketing and Health

The combined marketing strategies that are an emanation of concentrated corporate power have also exerted an influence on consumption and health. Evolving marketing strategies, epitomised by advertising, brand differentiation and other promotional techniques, have abetted the creation of wants, imagery and norms that stimulate drinking and, in certain cases, alcohol dependence.

At the core of alcohol marketing lies $2 billion in global advertising (1981) — a figure which is underestimated as it excludes a plethora of other promotional devices. Large TNC advertising complexes are by no means restricted to DMEs, but are deployed by TNCs in DEs, where rural consumers and new urban migrants are far more vulnerable to their allurements. Such a massive advertising barrage becomes the launching pad for new alcohol categories and brands, thereby generating new tastes, opening up new markets and assisting alcohol TNCs to compete much more effectively for the consumer's disposable income. Taking advantage of consumer heterogeneity according to sex, age, ethnic group, income and geographical groups, TNCs expand and annex markets by product differentiation and brand proliferation. Two demographic segments that have proved particularly vulnerable (in health terms) to these techniques have been women and youth.

Alcoholic-beverage-TNCs' targeting of women involves two corporate strategies applicable to all forms of market segmentation: generating new brands and redesigning older ones, both supported by large-scale advertising.[19] Such corporate strategies have played a prominent role in the growth of alcohol consumption and problems among women in several developed countries. Signs of these mounting problems are marked in the USA, where the advertising barrage has been the most intense and pervasive.[20] What makes these promotional efforts even more disturbing is growing medical evidence that women may develop liver cirrhosis from alcohol consumption faster than men, and that alcohol consumption by pregnant women is related to a range of foetal alcohol problems.[21]

While women's importance as consumers is unparalleled in size, the youth market assumes major importance for yet another reason. Laws against alcoholic beverage sales to adolescents exist in most developed countries. TNCs take this into account in formulating strategies aimed at persons reaching the legal drinking age. This is critical in terms of health as it is so very much easier to recruit non-drinkers (and the same applies to non-smokers) to a specific brand than a consumer whose loyalty is committed to another brand.

Buttressing the efficacy of traditional forms of advertising is a dazzling array of specific promotional techniques including free sampling, supporters clubs, logo merchandising, to designate but a few. It is in this context that public utterances by several alcohol TNCs on the merits of drinking in moderation should be scrutinised. Even on the assumption that such corporate contentions are made in good faith, their multi-billion dollar advertising outlays are anathema to the notion of moderate drinking. For what is at issue for the TNC is to maximise sales of, and profits from, the commodity in question.

**In a Few Words**

In tracing and analysing these complex corporate currents, it is by no means the intent of this book to document the serious social, economic and medical consequences of different levels of alcohol consumption. Research of this kind continues to be carried out by others. Rather, the book aims to demonstrate, on the basis of historical analysis, that transnational corporate structures and marketing strategies exercise an impact on the availability and consumption of alcoholic beverages in both developed and developing market economies.[22]

Such a statement is not to be construed mechanistically as suggesting a single causal relationship between corporate strategies and the consumption of alcoholic beverages. As with all commodities produced by corporations, alcohol consumption is a function of several interrelated factors. A leading contributory factor is the overall economic conjuncture of the world economy in general and of national economies in particular, inasmuch as they impinge on levels of income and employment of consumers. During the global recession of 1982 – 3, which left tens of millions unemployed, alcohol purchases declined in many countries despite rising promotional outlays of the alcohol TNCs.

Governments also exercise an impact on consumption in several legislative realms. Fiscal policies, embracing both direct and indirect taxation, can exercise a considerable influence on price and hence consumption of alcohol. The state is also in a position to intervene in the market with an array of measures that restrict alcohol availability as well as its promotion. Finally, the trajectory of alcohol consumption can be modified by different social institutions, for example religious and temperance organisations, youth movements, labour unions, women's organisations, etc., with all their diverse motives.

Hence, it is the complex complementary and adversarial interactions between TNCs and this configuration of economic, political and social forces which determine, in the last analysis, the volume, composition and patterns of alcohol consumption.

The state of scientific enquiry into these complex interrelationships as well as levels of alcohol production, consumption and trade, stands at highly differentiated levels for different countries and regions of the world. To be sure, for certain developing countries, relevant statistics on these and related demographic variables are either non-existent or parsimonious. The fragmentary evidence that exists, however, often reveals the magnitude of alcohol production and expenditures. In Thailand, for example, consumers spend nearly as much on alcoholic beverages as the government spends on oil imports. Thus, conclusions regarding the impact of TNCs on alcohol consumption in developing countries must, at best, be little more than a first approximation.

This book attempts to explore in depth one of the central forces within this mosaic, namely transnational corporate power. By mapping the transformation of alcohol corporations into conglomerates and national alcohol sectors into oligopolies, this work charts the movement of alcohol as a marketable commodity from the village pub of earlier centuries to the mega alcohol conglomerates of our time. Conceptually, this work brings into clearer perspective the twin movements of internationalisation and transnationalisation which are reshaping both the alcohol sector and all other commodity sectors on the world market.

The evolution of corporate power in alcohol is illustrative of four central movements that explain TNCs' shifting roles as they battle for global markets. By the early 1980s, this global market consisted of about $9 trillion of combined gross domestic products,[23] of which around $2.5 trillion was exported.

1.   The explosive growth of conglomerate extensions of the TNCs and further capital concentration in specific sectors to form oligopolies at national and international levels, have been conspicuous features of the last two decades.[24] The trajectory of the world market has been profoundly affected by the conglomerates' enhanced ability to undermine non-conglomerate competitors through their multi-product marketing networks, as well as through such increasingly sophisticated techniques as deploying profits from one product line to subsidise the pricing of another below the level of long-term total costs. The further surge to national and global oligopoly has not only reinforced the control of the TNCs over price formation, but has also offered an opportunity for more innovative collusive practices.

2.   These changes in corporate power structures have been accompanied by the introduction of a new set of corporate priorities. In the past two decades, there has been a marked transformation in the approach of TNCs to the entire productive chain. In practice, the extent of the ownership of TNCs over primary commodity output has shrunk and their control of processing, marketing, distribution and services has expanded. TNCs retained effective control of output through an ensemble of new techniques, of which contract growing in agriculture (including grapes for wine) is but one.[25]

3.   Corporate strategies in relation to the world market have likewise been conditioned by strides in science and technology, conspicuously in information services, transport and communications. TNCs have seized upon innovations in ways inconceivable a decade ago in order to fragment production processes around the world.

The institutional method chosen by them for this purpose has been to set up subsidiaries, joint ventures, licensing and subcontracting agreements.

4. These three trends have been underpinned by, and contributed to, a fourth: the internationalisation of finance through the growth in the number and importance of TNBs. Their rise has led to a very close relationship at the production and marketing levels between transnational banks, corporations, mega multi-commodity trading companies and certain segments of state power, with Japan exhibiting the most mature form of these relations.

These structural changes within international capitalism have influenced the beer, wine and spirits sectors in differing degrees of intensity over time. In this context, alcoholic beverages must be seen as a microcosm of the changes within global capitalism as a whole.

## Notes

1. For the purposes of this book a broad definition of health used by the World Health Organisation (WHO) is appropriate: 'Health is not only the absence of disease and infirmity, but also the presence of full psychological, mental, and social well-being.'

2. A TNC is any firm (industrial, agricultural, service, or any combination of these) which controls assets in two or more countries. There are approximately 18,000 around the world led by the US firm, Exxon, with 1981 sales of $115 billion.

3. Health and social problems related to excessive or inappropriate alcohol consumption are now widely recognised. Alcohol's role in cirrhosis of the liver, certain types of cancers, as well as such mental problems as psychotic disorders, depression and suicide has been documented. There is also convincing evidence of the significant role of alcohol in traffic accidents. In other areas, additional research is needed to assess the impact of alcohol on, for instance, failures in family and work roles, alcohol-related crime, work absenteeism, loss of productivity and industrial accidents.

4. US retail sales of alcoholic beverages totalled $40 billion in 1981. *New York Times*, 27 August 1982. Assuming alcoholic beverage prices to be at the US level in other DMEs, and one-half of the US level in developing countries, the global retail market for legal alcoholic beverages in market economies would be roughly $170 billion. Assuming prices to be one-fifth the US level in centrally planned economies (largely outside the TNC realm), their retail market would be roughly $10 billion.

5. See K. Bruun *et al., Alcohol Control Policies in Public Health Perspective* (The Finnish Foundation for Alcohol Studies, 1975). For an overview of literature on this relationship, see Ole-Jorgen Skog, 'Estimating Magnitudes and Trends of Alcohol-Related Problems: A Critical Appraisal' (National Institute for Alcohol Research, Oslo, 1982). See also, K. Mäkelä *et al., Alcohol, Society and the State*, Vol. 1 (Toronto, 1981); and WHO, *Problems Related to Alcohol Consumption*, Report of a WHO Expert Committee (Geneva, 1980).

6. The relationship between availability and consumption is very seldom a simple

one. While it is true that few available bottles of alcoholic beverages go unconsumed, what is far more revealing is the specific income group breakdown of consumption. In developing countries, for example, the numerically small, urban high-income groups and expatriates consume the largest proportion of alcoholic beverages made available through imports. Indeed, their share of consumption is higher for wine and distilled spirits than for beer. In sum, availability of specific alcoholic beverages in different countries has a highly differentiated impact on various consuming groups, an area ripe for future research.

7. In the USA, to take but one example, alcohol is involved in more than 66 per cent of homicides, 50 per cent of rapes, up to 70 per cent of assaults and 80 per cent of suicides. Center for Science in the Public Interests, *Alcohol Excise Tax Fact Sheet* (Washington DC, 1983).

8. To cite but one case, San Miguel Corporation in the Philippines currently distributes its beer (via its own trucking, barge and shipping fleets) to over 125,000 retail outlets throughout the archipelago.

9. Oligopoly defines a market dominated by a handful of firms whose corporate conduct is, at times, co-ordinated via such mechanisms as pricing policies that deviate from those which might prevail under more competitive conditions; various collusive practices; and a multiplicity of effective barriers against other firms aspiring to enter the sector.

10. For Guinness, this applies to its country of origin, Ireland, where it controls over 95 per cent of the market. In the UK, where it is now incorporated, it holds less than one-tenth.

11. Only in rare cases have governments applied antitrust legislation to slow this steady drive towards concentration.

12. Of over $10.1 billion legal global alcohol beverage imports in 1980, more than $1.3 billion was shipped into developing countries. The bulk of it was distilled spirits ($812 million), followed by wine ($293 million) and beer ($203 million).

13. For beer and distilled spirits TNCs, another major avenue of expansion has been the scaffolding of breweries and distilleries in developing countries, often in collaboration with members of the ruling oligarchies. Leading the field, Nigeria has contracted with TNCs for the erection of over ten breweries since 1978, with several more in the blueprint stage.

14. TNC sales of licenses to developing country entrepreneurs of brewery, winery and distillery technology has been spearheaded by the beer giants Heineken and United Breweries.

15. Computed from data supplied by the Addiction Research Foundation, Canada, 1982. Once again, rather than exercising restraint on these overseas flows, governmental policies have often augmented them through trade agreements favouring alcohol, and state aid to alcohol exporters. A prominent example is the Lomé Convention between EEC countries and a large group of Commonwealth nations that allows manufactured products from these former colonies, including Caribbean rum, to enter the EEC under preferential duties.

16. An informal geographical market-sharing arrangement between the three largest Mexican brewers has effectively carved the national market into three exclusive spheres, bestowing on each an area where promotional and distributional efforts are almost totally unhindered by competition.

17. A conglomerate is a corporation consisting of subsidiaries engaged in unrelated economic activities. Expansion of conglomerates takes place through mergers and takeovers.

18. For a thorough analysis of the transnational tobacco conglomerates, see United Nations Conference on Trade and Development (UNCTAD), *The Marketing and Distribution of Tobacco*, TD/B/C.1/205 (Geneva, 1978). A lesser tobacco TNC, Reemtsma in the FRG (now part of the Tchibo coffee empire), is also a major beer producer.

19. Particularly innovative in this realm has been Grand Metropolitan, which (through its International Distillers and Vintners (IDV) subsidiary) created the entirely new cream liqueur category aimed primarily at the female market.

20. About half of all global alcohol advertising dollars are spent on the US consumer. For a summary of recent studies on alcohol and women, see A. Lake, 'Alcoholism: Suddenly it's a young woman's problem', *Redbook* (June 1982).

21. The National Institute on Alcohol Abuse and Alcoholism (NIAAA) is carrying out research on this relationship. See ibid. The same is true of tobacco, as brought out by two WHO officials: 'Indeed, women who smoke are not only susceptible to the same respiratory pathology as men, to lung cancer, and to cardiovascular diseases, but in addition there is a smoking related pathology which is typical of women — e.g. pregnancy problems leading to the birth of smaller-for-date babies, and cardio-circulatory problems in women who both smoke and use oral contraceptives.' R. Masironi and L. Roy, 'Cigarette Smoking in Young Age Groups: Geographic Prevalence', *Heartbeat*, No. 2 (June 1982), p. 3.

22. The book does not purport to argue that corporations are the exclusive motive forces behind alcohol consumption, inasmuch as it existed prior to the advent of the TNC, and is present in Centrally Planned Economies (CPEs) in the absence of TNCs. The implication of this is that alcohol and alcohol problems have different cultural, political, economic and religious roots, particularly between market and planned economies, that merit separate enquiries.

23. This figure excludes the centrally planned economies. Frederick Clairmonte and John Cavanagh, 'Transnational Corporations and Services: The Final Frontier', *Trade and Development: An UNCTAD Review*, No. 5 (Geneva, 1984).

24. Prominent national oligopolies exist in several countries in the beer, distilled spirits, chemicals, pharmaceuticals, steel and food processing sectors, to name but a few. International oligopolies have become paramount in the past decade in petroleum, cigarettes, automobiles and numerous primary commodity trading sectors.

25. For a description of the role of contract growing in but one sector, see Randolf S. David *et al., Transnational Corporations and the Philippine Banana Export Industry* (Quezon City, 1981).

# PART ONE: STRUCTURE OF THE GLOBAL MARKET

# 1 A HISTORICAL OVERVIEW

The term 'alcohol' is of Arabic derivation, originally referring to any finely ground substance, and later coming to define the essential spirit of wine. All alcoholic beverages share a common base — the chemical compound ethyl alcohol,[1] an intoxicating agent. Another common denominator of all alcoholic beverages is that they are drugs, endowed with the capacity to influence physical, mental and social behaviour. The colossal diversity of raw material inputs used in the production of the three specific categories of alcoholic beverages — wine, beer and distilled spirits — spans practically the entire spectrum of fruits and vegetables.

## Wine

Earliest historical records indicate that wine and beer were the first alcoholic beverages to be invented. Since fruit and berry wines are easier to produce than beer, it is often inferred that wine was the first to make its début. While the bulk of wine is made from the grape's fermented juice, it can also be produced from other commodities, for example rice in Asia and palm tree sap in Africa.[2] Geographically, wine making has been primarily confined to temperate regions. Classification of different wines is based on the grape's varietal or species characteristics, including flavours, colour and chemical composition, and on processing methods.

Some of the earliest historical records on the transformation of grapes into wine (viticulture) date back to 2500 BC in Egypt. The Old Testament traces the early significance of the wine industry in other areas of the Middle East. The propagation of classical Hellenic and Hellenistic civilisation led to its widespread production and marketing in colonies in an area extending from the Black Sea to the Spanish peninsula. Grape growing and wine making were further extended into the Rhine, Moselle and Danube valleys by the Roman legions. Wine's expansion was to be furthered by the role that it assumed in religious ritual after the collapse of the Roman Empire, via the monastic orders. With the Renaissance discoveries of the sixteenth century, wine making broke the confines of the Old World

15

and spread to Mexico, South America, South Africa, Australia and California.

## Beer

It would appear that beer was the second alcoholic beverage to make its début on the historic stage.[3] Like wine, beer can be fabricated from a variety of raw materials: millet, maize, sorghum, barley, wheat, rice, etc. Brewing is the basic manufacturing process, consisting of three phases: soaking the grain in water; boiling it, in most cases with hops; and finally, fermentation.[4]

One of the world's oldest historical documents is a clay tablet from Babylonia dating from around 6000 BC, revealing the preparation of beer for sacrificial purposes.[5] Already 2000 years later, it is believed that Babylonians brewed 16 different kinds of beer from barley, wheat and honey.[6] Records from around 2100 BC described Sumerian and Babylonian medicine men as promoters of its alleged medicinal properties.[7]

The first precise historical record on beer's overseas trade is found in Pliny's *History of the Ancient World*, where it is reported that the techniques of beer production spread from Egypt to Greece, from whence it was diffused to other Mediterranean countries. Beer-making techniques came later with the Romans to northern and western Europe in areas where viticulture had not become generalised.[8] Beer was first introduced into Bavaria in AD 736, a region destined to become one of the major world centres of the industry in later centuries. It was in Europe during the eighth century that a new era of beer making began with the introduction of bittering agents, principally hops.[9]

From the end of the twelfth century, with the growth of urban centres in England, simple commercial operations were set up in which brewing and marketing were carried out in the same building. These brewing houses gradually replaced monasteries as the central brewing institution of the Middle Ages.[10] By the fourteenth century the great brewing houses of Germany were already the source of substantial exports.

Although it had become a popular beverage in both rural and urban areas, beer was given a major boost with the rise of the industrial revolution in the last quarter of the eighteenth century, which witnessed the advent of the large-scale commercial brewery. It was, however, only in the early twentieth century that beer marketing and distribution broke the fetters of limited geographical areas. With the emergence of massive economies of scale, leading to a drop in unit costs of production and the creation of brand names and advertising, marketing was to acquire a national and then an international character.

## Distilled Spirits

Stemming from their relative technical complexity, distilled spirits were invented independently and in several countries very much later than wine and beer. The technique, which has not altered appreciably over the centuries, involves the concentration of ethyl alcohol by distilling an already fermented product. Essentially, this process consists of vaporising the alcohol in the fermented product, thus separating it from the original liquid. Alcohol is then recondensed into a liquid of enhanced potency.

From extant records, it appears that the Chinese were among the pioneers, distilling rice beer into a stronger beverage (c. 800 BC). Similar techniques were also discovered in Southern Asia, the Middle East and elsewhere, with inputs of raw materials that varied widely by region (Table 1.1).

## Table 1.1: Origins of Various Distilled Spirits

| | Date | Inputs[a] | Fermented liquor | Distillate |
|---|---|---|---|---|
| China | — | rice and millet | tchoo | sautchoo |
| Ceylon and India | 800 BC | rice and molasses or palm sap | toddy | arrack |
| Asiatic Tatary | — | cow's milk | kefir | arika |
| Caucasia | — | mare's milk | koumiss | skhou |
| Japan | — | rice | sake | sochu |
| Britain | AD 500 | honey | mead | mead distilled |
| Italy | 1000 | grapes | wine | brandy |
| Ireland | 1100 | oats and barley malt | beer | usquebaugh |
| Spain | 1200 | grapes | wine | *aqua vini* |
| France | 1300 | grapes | wine | cognac |
| Scotland | 1500 | malted barley | beer | *aqua vitae*, whisky |

Note: a. These are the major inputs, which are by no means exhaustive.
Source: *Encyclopaedia Brittanica*, section on 'Distilled Liquor'.

Early distilled spirits were processed primarily from sugar-based products, mainly grapes and honey. In the late Middle Ages, starchy grains flourished as a raw material ingredient. By the mid-seventeenth century, consumption of grain-based distilled spirits had grown so extensively that it engendered widespread government control in several countries.

By the early nineteenth century, technology had advanced to a point where large-scale continuous stills had come into existence in western Europe, with operations which remain basically similar to current production technology. With modernisation of technology moving in tandem with growing consumption, state and municipal authorities came to play a far greater role in control over production, marketing and revenue collection.

## Notes

1. In addition to being the basic ingredient of alcoholic beverages, ethyl alcohol is also used as a food solvent, and in pharmaceuticals, toiletries and cosmetics.

2. Other fruits can be fermented to produce a kind of wine, which is usually designated by the name of the fruit, as in peach wine, blackberry wine, etc.

3. For an historical overview, see H. A. Monckton, *A History of English Beer and Ale* (London, 1966); and James Robertson, *The Great American Beer Book* (Ottawa, 1978).

4. Chemically, beer is produced from the action of yeast, bacteria or fungus on grain sugar or plant starch. The sugar is converted into alcohol and carbon dioxide by this fermentation process, and beer is the end product. A 1981 breakdown of the raw material inputs revealed the following breakdown by volume: malt (77 per cent); sugar (13); other cereals (9); and hops (1). The Brewers Society, *Beer Facts* (London, 1982). Often ignored by public health workers is the high percentage of sugar.

5. Ancient China and Japan were also among the first countries to record the invention of beer, originally from millet and subsequently from rice. Another early beer whose precise origins are lost in the mists of time is the Southern African sorghum-based beer, kaffir. The appearance of a barley-based beer was also noted in Ancient Egypt where legend speaks of the God of agriculture, Isiris, teaching humans to prepare beer. As with wine, its origins were said to be divine. Egyptian doctors around 1400 BC were including both beer and wine in about 15 per cent of their prescriptions.

6. Robertson, p. 15.

7. It was estimated that, in certain years, up to 40 per cent of the Sumerian grain crop was used for brewing. See Herman Ronnenberg, 'Beer in the Cradle of Civilization', *Brewers Digest* (December 1980).

8. The Roman's word for beer, *cerevisia*, is derived from 'Ceres', the Goddess of agriculture, and *vis*, strength.

9. Hops are the dried ripe cones of a vine member of the nettle family. The resin or extract from the cones is used for beer preservation and bittering, adding a tangy or sharp taste to the brew.

10. During the Middle Ages in Europe, Christian clergymen were often the principal beer wholesalers, while the Jews were the major retailers. See Robertson, p. 17.

# 2 OUTPUT, TRADE AND CONSUMPTION

With few exceptions, stemming largely from religious bans, output and trade of alcoholic beverages have ramified to all corners of the earth. In recent decades, propagation of alcoholic beverages has been wrought not only by increased trade flows, but also by increasing capital flows via licensing agreements and the implantation abroad of subsidiaries and joint ventures, which are some of the major instruments of penetration by TNCs. Capital flows are much more difficult to quantify, and are examined in detail in subsequent chapters on TNC strategies. Up to the present, these capital movements have assumed their greatest importance in the beer sector (particularly in developing countries), and to a lesser extent in wine and distilled spirits.

Trade and output figures are more easily measured than capital flows and are a fairly accurate gauge of the availability of alcoholic beverages. However, they should be analysed with one important caveat. Non-commercial and illicit production and trade, quite substantial in many cases, are excluded from the figures. 'In many developing countries,' as WHO noted, 'in fact, unrecorded home production may be the main source of alcoholic beverages and little is known about the quantities available.'[1] The importance of home production has, however, been mitigated by increases in alcohol trade flows. A salient feature of alcoholic beverage output has been the increasing prominence of commercial beverages over traditional ones in developing countries, stimulated by the flourishing traffic in both legal and illegal alcohol.

The increasing importance of TNC-produced commercial beverages as opposed to traditional ones is also evidenced in DMEs. Japanese data indicate that over the past decade output of sake, the major traditional beverage, has stagnated while beer and whisky have surged ahead. Between 1971 and 1981, sake's share of domestic alcoholic beverage output fell from 31 to 22 per cent, while that of beer rose from 60 to 67 per cent, and that of whisky from 3 to 5 per cent. These shifting output and consumption patterns are indicative of a trend seen also in several developing countries: consumption of traditional beverages in the countryside coupled with a growth of TNC-produced beverages in urban areas.

Another major determinant of alcoholic beverage availability is numbers and distribution of retail and drinking outlets, and regulations concerning time, place and quantity of sales. This varies markedly between countries depending on retail sector concentration and governmental control.[2]

## Output

### Beer[3]

Commercial beer output worldwide has been estimated to have more than doubled from 407 million hectolitres in 1960 to 911 million in 1980. More than four-fifths of this output is in the developed countries, where the statistical base is the most reliable. Over the past two decades, there has been a clear shift in regional distribution of output, with the share of all developed regions falling, and that of developing regions rising. Overall, Latin American, Asian and African commercial output during this time span rose from 55 million to over 220 million hectolitres, a jump of over 400 per cent.[4] By 1980, developing countries as a whole had captured 18.3 per cent of global commercial output.

Out of 46 countries where commercial output grew over 50 per cent from 1973 to 1980, 42 were developing countries; out of 17 where beer output actually rocketed over 100 per cent, 16 were developing countries.[5] China led the world with output growth of 243 per cent (1975 – 80), and certain TNC brewing executives predict a quadrupling of Chinese beer output in the 1980s.[6]

### Wine[7]

Wine's ascent over the past two decades has been less dramatic, with output growing annually at 1.7 per cent, less than half of commercial beer's yearly rise of 4.1 per cent. The Asian and Australasia/Oceania regions recorded the highest growth, but still represent negligible forces on the global market. Wine's historic centre remains Europe, where four out of every five bottles are produced. Latin and North America fall in place behind Europe, based almost entirely on output from Argentina and the United States. The major regional shift over the two decades has been the halving of Africa's output. Again, one country is largely responsible: Algeria's wine volume plummeted from 16 to 3 million hectolitres between 1960 and 1980, with the departure of many European settlers and the substantial shift of resources from agriculture to industry.

Behind European wine dominance stands the trio of Italy, France and Spain, which have produced almost three-fifths of global wine over these two decades. Among the top six producers, the USSR and the USA have massively expanded wine making, which may portend a narrowing of the gap between themselves and the big three.

The myriad of raw materials used in beer and distilled spirits renders estimates of land area reserved for alcohol inputs hazardous. This is not the case for wine production, however, where around 35 million acres of the planet's cropland are allocated to wine grapes.

## Distilled Spirits[8]

Distilled spirits are a highly heterogeneous category, comprising the whisky family (including bourbon, rye, blends, etc.), white spirits (rum, gin,[9] vodka[10]), brandy and liqueurs. Because of this great diversity, statistics on global distilled spirits output are still of a highly unequal nature, preventing any accurate comparison of 1960 and 1980.

Statistics from the Addiction Research Foundation in Toronto, however, offer a glimpse of global trends since 1970. A 1977 regional breakdown of distilled spirits reveals striking similarities with the 1980 beer breakdown: in both categories, Europe accounts for half of the output, North America for over a fifth, with both Africa and Oceania negligible factors in world production. Concentration is marked within two regions: Japan and the Republic of Korea account for over two-thirds of Asian output; Brazil and Argentina for well over three-quarters of Latin America's.

Over the 1970s, three countries have consistently accounted for almost two-fifths of global production: USA, USSR and UK. Among the top ten, the fastest growers (1970 – 7) were a DE (Korea) and a Centrally Planned Economy (CPE) (Poland), with a fall also recorded in a CPE (USSR) and a DE (Brazil). Six DMEs fall in between these two extremes, led by France with a 60 per cent growth over the seven-year span. Apart from Brazil and South Korea, three other DEs surpassed the 50 thousand kilolitre mark (1977, measured in absolute alcohol): India, Argentina and Malaysia. Of all distilled spirits, the whisky group is by far the leading category, and exhibits marked geographical concentration. Nine out of every ten litres are bottled in four countries: the UK (34 per cent), the USA (26 per cent), Canada (15 per cent), and Japan (14 per cent).[11]

**Trade Concentration**

Legal exports of alcoholic beverages surpassed $9.4 billion in 1980, of which slightly under half was comprised of wine ($4.6 billion); two-fifths were distilled alcoholic beverages ($3.7 billion); and one-tenth was beer ($1.1 billion). In each of these three sub-groups concentration is marked, with a few countries encompassing the bulk of exports (Table 2.1): France and Italy together control almost three-fifths of wine exports; the UK and France, a commanding four-fifths of distilled alcoholic beverages; and the Netherlands, the FRG and Denmark around half of beer exports. Overall, three-fifths of alcoholic beverage exports emanate from France, the UK and Italy.

Table 2.1:   Alcoholic Beverages: World's Ten Largest Exporters, 1980 ($000,000)

| Country | Total alcoholic beverages | | Wine | | Distilled alcoholic beverages | | Beer | |
|---|---|---|---|---|---|---|---|---|
| | exports | % | exports | % | exports | % | exports | % |
| France | 2,822 | 30.0 | 1,775 | 38.5 | 1,005 | 27.3 | 42 | 3.7 |
| UK | 2,041 | 21.7 | 57 | 1.2 | 1,940 | 52.7 | 44 | 3.9 |
| Italy | 1,000 | 10.6 | 919 | 19.9 | 77 | 2.1 | 4 | 0.4 |
| FRG | 547 | 5.8 | 345 | 7.5 | 33 | 0.9 | 169 | 14.6 |
| Spain | 458 | 4.9 | 404 | 8.8 | 50 | 1.4 | 4 | 0.4 |
| Netherlands | 364 | 3.9 | 6 | 0.1 | 66 | 1.8 | 292 | 26.0 |
| Canada | 345 | 3.6 | 1 | 0.0 | 267 | 7.3 | 77 | 6.9 |
| Portugal | 244 | 2.6 | 240 | 5.2 | 2 | 0.0 | 2 | 0.2 |
| Bulgaria | 179 | 1.9 | 179 | 3.9 | n.a.[a] | n.a. | 0 | 0.0 |
| Hungary | 160 | 1.7 | 160 | 3.5 | n.a. | n.a. | 0 | 0.0 |
| Others | 1,256 | 13.3 | 528 | 11.4 | n.a. | n.a. | 493 | 43.9 |
| Total | 9,416 | 100.0 | 4,614 | 100.0 | 3,680 | 100.0 | 1,127 | 100.0 |

Note: a. Not available.
Source: Computed from data in International Trade Centre data bank, 1982; and Food and Agriculture Organization (FAO), *Trade Yearbook 1980* (Rome, 1981).

Imports are almost as concentrated as exports, with the top ten absorbing 76 per cent of imports versus the top ten's 87 per cent export share (Table 2.2). France, the UK and the FRG are among the top five in both imports and exports. The paramount force in all categories of alcoholic beverage imports is the USA which, along with the FRG and the UK, controls 45 per cent of total alcoholic beverage imports. The same three countries also account for over two-fifths of wine and distilled spirits imports, while the USA and France account for almost half of beer imports.

Table 2.2:   Alcoholic Beverages: World's Ten Largest
Importers, 1980 ($000,000)

| Country | Total alcoholic beverages | | Wine | | Distilled alcoholic beverages | | Beer | |
|---|---|---|---|---|---|---|---|---|
| | imports | % | imports | % | imports | % | imports | % |
| USA | 2,408 | 23.7 | 785 | 15.3 | 1,196 | 30.8 | 427 | 37.7 |
| FRG | 1,137 | 11.2 | 761 | 14.9 | 339 | 8.7 | 37 | 3.3 |
| UK | 1,001 | 9.9 | 661 | 12.9 | 257 | 6.6 | 83 | 7.3 |
| USSR | 683 | 6.7 | 648 | 12.6 | n.a.[a] | n.a. | 35 | 3.1 |
| France | 614 | 6.0 | 332 | 6.5 | 156 | 4.0 | 126 | 11.1 |
| Belgium-Lux | 535 | 5.3 | 354 | 6.9 | 136 | 3.5 | 45 | 4.0 |
| Netherlands | 383 | 3.8 | 278 | 5.4 | 94 | 2.4 | 11 | 1.0 |
| Japan | 337 | 3.3 | 62 | 1.2 | 265 | 6.8 | 10 | 1.4 |
| Switzerland | 322 | 3.2 | 277 | 5.4 | 21 | 0.5 | 24 | 2.1 |
| Italy | 293 | 2.9 | 91 | 1.8 | 138 | 3.6 | 64 | 5.6 |
| Others | 2,430 | 24.0 | 874 | 17.1 | n.a. | n.a. | 266 | 23.4 |
| Total | 10,143 | 100.0 | 5,123 | 100.0 | 3,886 | 100.0 | 1,134 | 100.0 |

Note: a. Not available.
Source: Computed from data in International Trade Centre data bank, 1982; and
FAO, *Trade Yearbook 1980* (Rome, 1981).

While there were no developing countries among the ten leading
alcoholic beverage importers or exporters, certain developing
countries are spending considerable sums on imports. Developing
countries spent $293 million on wine imports in 1980, with the Ivory
Coast and Brazil accounting for close to one-sixth of the total.[12] One
of the fastest growing importing regions is Africa, with 23 countries
importing an average of 2 million bottles of French champagne
yearly (1982) at a cost of around $40 million.[13]

The other major alcohol sector where developing country imports
rose rapidly over the past two decades is distilled spirits. By 1980,
three imported over $50 million: Venezuela, Hong Kong and Singa-
pore. Trinidad and Tobago, with a population of merely 1.1 million,
spent $40 million on whisky imports alone in 1982, or $36 *per
capita.*[14]

While DE imports have showed a steady increase since the
mid-1950s, they have been subject to fluctuations determined by the
overall state of the world economy. In 1983, for example, many
countries were compelled to cut back alcohol imports because of
foreign exchange shortages.

**Consumption**

Europe, the Americas and Australasia, with less than a quarter of
the world's population, consume four-fifths of recorded alcoholic
beverages. Europe alone, with only one-eighth of the planet's
population, consumes around one-half.[15] Over the last two decades,
both overall and *per capita* consumption of alcoholic beverages has
increased in many countries. Noteworthy are the considerable
variations in countries of different cultural origins. Out of 50
countries surveyed in 1980, *per capita* consumption (measured in
litres of pure alcohol) ranged from 0.2 litres in Lebanon to 18.4 in
Luxembourg.[16] Barring Hungary and Argentina, the top ten *per
capita* consuming countries are all West European. As figures
measure only commercial beverage consumption, however, they are
biased against developing countries, where the highest proportions
of unrecorded and illicit output occur.

Variations in the *per capita* consumption growth among the top 20
consuming countries are likewise marked. Average *per capita* consumption growth (1960 – 80) ranged from – 0.8 per cent in France to
6.3 per cent in the Netherlands (Table 2.3).[17] While revealing, these
*per capita* figures often mask substantial differences in drinking
patterns within countries by age, race, social class, religion and
occupation. According to *Le Monde*, there has been a shift in the
social class nature of French wine consumption in recent years.
Consumption of table wine, largely accounted for by the working
class, is diminishing, whereas that of quality wine, principally
consumed by middle and upper income groups, has risen.[18] Likewise, countries differ widely in the relative numbers of abstainers,
resulting in equally marked country variations in percentages of
heavy drinkers and the incidence of alcohol-related problems.[19]

A paucity of developing country data inhibits detailed analysis of
consumption patterns. Output figures examined earlier pointed to
huge increases in beer production in DEs over the past two decades
and, since very little is exported, it can be surmised that consumption
has likewise advanced rapidly. A sampling of consumption trends
between 1960 and 1980 in 14 Latin American and Northern African
countries bears this out. *Per capita* beer consumption rose in 10 out
of 14 countries, led by Paraguay with a jump of 503 per cent.

In three countries with comparable data spirits consumption rose,
while wine grew in only four out of ten. Data are even more fragmentary in the two DE regions where output data suggest that consump-

Table 2.3: Alcoholic Beverages: *Per Capita* Consumption, 1980

| Country | Total (litres, pure alcohol) | | Average annual percentage change 1960 – 80 | Beer (litres) | | Wine (litres) | | Spirits (litres, pure alcohol) | |
|---|---|---|---|---|---|---|---|---|---|
| Luxembourg | (1)[a] | 18.4 | 4.1 | (8) | 121.0 | (6) | 48.2 | (1) | 9.0 |
| France | (2) | 14.8 | – 0.8 | | 49.3 | (1) | 95.4 | | 2.5 |
| Spain | (3) | 14.1 | 2.6 | | 53.4 | (5) | 64.7 | (10) | 3.0 |
| Italy | (4) | 13.0 | 0.3 | | 16.7 | (2) | 93.0 | | 1.9 |
| FRG | (5) | 12.7 | 3.1 | (1) | 145.7 | | 25.6 | (8) | 3.1 |
| Hungary | (6) | 11.5 | 3.1 | | 86.3 | | 35.0 | (3) | 4.5 |
| Argentina | (7) | 11.4 | 0.8 | | 7.7 | (3) | 75.0 | | 2.0 |
| Austria | (8) | 11.0 | 1.2 | | 101.9 | (10) | 35.8 | | 1.6 |
| Portugal | (9) | 11.0 | 0.04 | | 33.8 | (4) | 70.0 | | 0.9 |
| Belgium | (10) | 10.8[b] | 2.7 | (5) | 131.3 | | 20.6 | | 2.4 |
| Switzerland | (11) | 10.5 | 0.3 | | 69.0 | (7) | 47.4 | | 2.1 |
| Australia[b] | (12) | 9.8 | 2.1 | (4) | 134.3 | | 17.4 | | 1.0 |
| GDR | (13) | 9.7 | 3.8 | (3) | 135.0 | | 9.5 | (4) | 4.5 |
| New Zealand | (14) | 9.7 | 2.0 | (9) | 118.0 | | 11.0 | | 2.5 |
| Czechoslovakia | (15) | 9.6 | 2.8 | (2) | 137.8 | | 15.5 | (5) | 3.5 |
| Denmark | (16) | 9.2 | 4.9 | (7) | 121.5 | | 14.0 | | 1.5 |
| Canada[b] | (17) | 9.1 | 3.2 | | 87.6 | | 8.5 | (6) | 3.4 |
| Netherlands | (18) | 8.8 | 6.3 | | 86.4 | | 12.9 | | 2.7 |
| Poland | (19) | 8.7 | 4.2 | | 30.4 | | 10.1 | (2) | 6.0 |
| USA | (20) | 8.7 | 3.0 | | 92.0 | | 7.9 | (9) | 3.1 |

Notes: a. Figures in parentheses indicate ranking.
b. For year 1979/80.
Source: Computed from figures of *Produktschap voor Gedistilleerde Dranken* (1981); and data supplied by WHO.

tion has grown fastest: Sub-Saharan Africa and Asia. In Zambia, for example, *per capita* consumption of commercial alcoholic beverages jumped from 42 to 150 litres (1961 – 76), a growth rate that can perhaps be extrapolated to certain other African countries.[20]

Consumption patterns, when translated into their drain on disposable income, indicate the magnitude of expenditures incurred in alcohol use and abuse. According to the US Department of Agriculture (USDA), inhabitants of certain countries spend up to 13 per cent of disposable income on alcohol, with Ireland (12.6 per cent), Hungary (11.6) and Poland (11.5) at the top of the list.[21] Reliable data indicating changes in alcohol expenditures over time exist for only a handful of countries. In the UK, alcoholic beverages as a percentage of total household expenditure rose from 3.2 in 1960 to 4.8 in 1980.[22] There is a marked variation in alcohol expenditure between lower and higher income groups: in a breakdown of 16 income groups, the poorest four spent under 3.2 per cent on alcohol, while the richest three all spent 5.4 per cent. The lower and middle income groups are also recorded as spending around twice as much on beer as wine and spirits, whereas wealthier groups spent only a little more on beer.[23]

Expressed in money terms, alcohol consumption levels can attain staggering dimensions. By 1979, the average Japanese spent the equivalent of $222 yearly on alcoholic beverages, slightly trailing the $249 of his US counterpart.[24]

## Beverage Substitution

Analysis focused exclusively on alcoholic beverages gives a distorted image, since they are but one major grouping of liquids which, on the surface, 'compete' for consumer expenditures. What is of the essence, however, is that liquids themselves do not compete with one another. Rather, it is corporations producing and marketing them that compete for ever larger market shares.

This distinction on the nature of competition is basic because it indicates primarily that the trajectory of alcoholic beverages is determined by the configuration of corporate forces (and their relative revenues, levels of concentration, advertising muscle, etc.) in all competing beverage groups. To view competition through the prism of corporate power, structures and strategies is even more important, inasmuch as certain corporations produce and market a wide variety of beverages. The Coca Cola Company is illustrative of the ramifications of diversification since it is one of the market leaders in soft drinks, fruit juices and wine.

Although global beverage consumption data are non-existent, partial data provide some insights into consumption patterns in certain DMEs. What they highlight is the marked variations between countries. In the USA, soft drinks is the paramount beverage group, whereas, in the FRG, coffee is the leader.[25] Such patterns of consumption have very little to do with relative prices, as evidenced in the consumption of tea (the cheapest beverage per litre after water) which, in both countries, ranks fifth.[26]

Far more telling are relative concentration levels in each grouping. In most countries, both alcoholic beverages and soft drinks are highly concentrated sectors in production, processing and market—

ing. Coffee, cocoa and tea (essentially tropical-based beverages) are highly concentrated only in processing and marketing. They are, conversely (except for tea), highly fragmented in production, which is largely within the orbit of small-scale producers.

Fruit juices and milk, the other two major beverage groups, while presently less concentrated, are increasingly being pulled into the TNCs processing and marketing orbit. Water, which historically constituted a major non-price competitor to these beverages, is also falling prey to corporate forces. In the early 1980s, food and beverage giants, such as Coca Cola, Foremost-McKesson and Beatrice Foods, followed in the wake of Great Waters of France (Perrier) into bottled water, and now dominate a rapidly mushrooming $550 million US bottled water market.[27]

Mustering gallonage growth is the battleground on which these corporate groupings deploy their forces. Up to the present, all have made inroads on the water market; and certain beverage groupings are making inroads on others. In the USA, for example, the major growth points projected for the 1980s are soft drinks and beer, which also happen to be two of the most concentrated sectors.[28] Also in the USA, alcoholic beverages boosted their share of total beverage consumption from 15 per cent in 1960 to 21 per cent in 1978, and this is projected to rise to 25 per cent by 1990.[29]

This upsurge in US alcoholic beverage consumption is indicative of global alcoholic trends and is also reflected in global alcohol exports of almost $10 billion (1980), second among beverages only to coffee.

Alcohol substitutability has relevance in other fields, namely industrial fuels. In earlier times, farm commodities such as maize and sugar cane were used primarily for food. Later, they found wider applications in the manufacture of alcoholic beverages. More recently, and this could very well represent a novel technological wave, alcohol derived from these commodities is being transformed into industrial fuels. While the chemistry of these processes was uncovered in the nineteenth century, it was the oil shock of 1973 that spurred their industrial applications.

Indubitably, large-scale industrial alcohol is already making an impact on the alcoholic beverage industry by providing outlets for surplus capacity. Three large breweries, Heileman (USA), Olympia (USA) and Allied-Lyons (UK), are now converting breweries to manufacture fuel grade alcohol. One of the major ingredients for this industrial alcohol will be their surplus beer. Likewise in the wine sector, the European Economic Community (EEC) authorises around one-fifth of all EEC wine (1980 – 1) to be recycled through distillation into industrial alcohol, thereby attenuating the wine surplus.[30]

In certain DEs, large-scale industrial alcohol ventures may exercise a different impact on alcoholic beverages. Brazil and the Philippines are investing over $100 million each in plants to distil industrial alcohol from sugar. Under certain conditions, this could push up sugar prices that would affect the price of sugar-based alcoholic beverages.[31]

## Illicit Alcohol

The foregoing statistical overview of alcoholic beverages is in no way designed to give an exhaustive picture of their output, trade and consumption. Missing in this picture is the large and highly lucrative traffic in illicit alcohol on national and global markets.[32] In many cases, tax structures and rigorous governmental control over distribution circuits provide the motive force for the internationalisation of illicit trafficking.

Understandably, no accurate estimates exist on the extent of global output and trade flows in illicit alcohol. Just as licit trade flows in alcoholic beverages have grown enormously over the last two decades, it can be surmised that this growing market has also been nourished by the illicit traffic. Faced with critical foreign exchange constraints and rising levels of indebtedness, the bulk of developing countries are becoming more vulnerable to relatively cheaper illicit imports, with a disproportionate amount of them being absorbed by higher income groups.

Illustrative of the forces that are fuelling this illicit traffic is Brazil. Due to extremely high traffic barriers, symptomatic of many developing countries, a case of standard Scotch whisky bottles sold f.o.b. (free on board) in the UK for £17 cost the equivalent of £266 in Brazil in 1981. In such a context, it is not surprising that large quantities of whisky are smuggled into Brazil from Paraguay, where a flourishing black market prevails, allegedly dominated by four major traffickers.[33]

As against Venezuela's 1976 legal imports of 28 million litres of alcoholic beverages, it is estimated that between 1 million and 10 million litres were illegally imported.[34] As the realm of profit becomes larger, it can be expected that concentration will be speeded up among the global traffickers whose marketing circuits are already globalised, thus increasing their capacity to bypass government control. It should be added that international illicit traffic is almost entirely confined to distilled alcoholic beverages because of their very high prices and margins, as well as the limited number of distilleries in developing countries.[35]

International illicit traffic is by no means the sole preserve of DEs. Certain Spanish traders were arrested in 1981 for importing ethyl alcohol suitable for human consumption under the false labelling of denatured alcohol for industrial use. The commercial logic behind this illicit traffic was the lower import duties on industrial alcohol, merchandised at about a half the price of domestic grape-based alcohol.[36]

The scale of global illicit traffic is matched, and possibly surpassed, by illicit indigenous production and marketing networks. While, once again, precise numbers are unavailable, such traffic occurs in all major regions. In developing countries, it assumes tragic dimensions in view of the often lethal consequences of bootleg alcohol. Recently, in India, at least 345 persons from Bangalore and Mysore died from bootleg alcohol poisoning.

According to the *International Herald Tribune*, a popular Indian bootleg brand, appropriately named 'black lightning', is concocted as follows: 'Take a handful of rotten fruit. Mix in bark from a nearby tree, some coarse brown sugar, chicken droppings and old shoes to speed up the fermentation process. Boil it up and add methyl alcohol for extra kick.'[37] Its price is around the equivalent of $0.25 a bottle, about a quarter of the price of the cheapest legal liquor.

In New Delhi alone, it has been claimed that 5,000 gallons of bootleg alcohol are peddled daily, mainly to low-income workers unable to afford legal alcohol. According to other reports from Bangalore, bootlegging business has scaled such heights that over 10,000 persons distribute illegal liquor to about 500 shops (three times the number of licensed bars). Yearly revenues from this traffic are believed to top the equivalent of $80 million and this in the Bangalore region exclusively. For the sub-continent as a whole, this implies that illicit alcohol has become a multi-million dollar industry.

'Black lightning' finds its counterparts in almost all developing countries, of which Malaysia's 'Samsu' is but another. Despite legislation against its brewers and distributors, according to the Consumer Association of Penang, 'illicit Samsu is still being sold to anyone who wants it'.[38] And this, five months after 32 people died and several others were blinded by it, again with its hapless victims being mainly from lower income groups.

Traffic in illicit alcohol assumes different dimensions in developed countries. In the USA, for example, illicit output has plummeted markedly over the past half decade. The post-prohibition illegal stills closed down by the Federal Government topped 16,700 in 1935; by 1975 the number of closures dropped to 721, and by 1979 reached an all-time low of 40. According to the chemical branch chief of the now defunct US Bureau of Alcohol, Tobacco and Firearms, 'as the cost of yeast, sugar and copper increase, the making of illicit spirits will become less profitable and decline further'.[39]

To this list could be added the costs of competing with giant conglomerates in an age of high interest rates and economies of scale. While bootleg output may drop with the elimination of one group of actors, bootleg distribution flourishes with the growing sophistication of another set of actors: liquor hijackers.

These hijackers embrace the mafia and others impelled by two basic considerations: highly differential liquor taxes between states; and a favourable marketing vantage point of many hijackers, whose ramifications proliferate into such liquor distribution outlets as casinos, bars, houses of prostitution, etc. The extent of this hijacking can be gauged from FBI estimates that liquor is the nation's most frequently hijacked commodity, trailed by cigarettes and jeans.[40] The USA is by no means the exception among developed countries. As much as 12 per cent of alcohol consumption in Norway, for example, is in the form of illicitly produced, or privately imported, spirits.[41] Illicit traffic in alcoholic beverages is certain to continue as long as import duties on beverages vary widely from country to country.

## Notes

1. Joy Moser, *Prevention of Alcohol-related Problems* (Toronto, 1980), published on behalf of the World Health Organization by the Alcoholism and Drug Addiction Research Foundation, p. 39.
2. This is examined in a subsequent section on retailing.
3. Commercial beer figures are computed from data in: Finnish Foundation for

Alcohol Studies and World Health Organization Regional Office For Europe, *International Statistics on Alcoholic Beverages* (Finland, 1977); and Joh. Barth & Sohn of Nuremberg, 1981.

4. Excludes Japan and South Africa.

5. Computed from figures of Joh. Barth & Sohn of Nuremberg, 1981; see *World Drinks Report* (18 August 1981), for complete listing.

6. *Financial Times*, 6 January 1982. To get a sense of the potential of China's beer market, Chinese *per capita* consumption is 0.6 litres per year as against 147 litres in the FRG. *Far Eastern Economic Review*, 22 January 1982.

7. Commercial wine statistics are computed from data in: Finnish Foundation for Alcohol Studies and World Health Organization Regional Office For Europe (1977); and Food and Agriculture Organization (FAO), *Production Yearbook 1980* (Rome, 1981).

8. Spirits data are computed from data of the Addiction Research Foundation, 1982.

9. Gin distilling orginated in Holland in the sixteenth century and the name 'gin' is derived from the Dutch word for juniper, *geneva*. The traditional method of producing London Distilled Dry Gin uses alcohol which has been rectified (redistilled for added purity) at a strength of at least 96 per cent alcohol by volume. This is redistilled in the presence of juniper berries, coriander seed and other botanicals appropriate to each distiller's formula. The gin manufacturer uses specialised stills for this process, the product of the redistillation being about 80 per cent alcohol by volume, which is then reduced to a bottling strength of between 38 and 47 per cent alcohol by volume by the addition of demineralised water. See National Economic Development Council (NEDC), *Distilling: Scotch Whisky* (London, 1978).

10. Vodka can be made from many kinds of agricultural raw materials. In the West it is usually produced from molasses or grain; and in East Europe from grain, rice or potatoes. Specially designed stills are used to distil high strength (not less than 96 per cent alcohol by volume) spirits which are then selected by individual producers. After the prime distillation, the spirit is treated with activated carbon to obtain characteristics required by individual producers and is compounded with approved materials before reduction to bottling strength between 37.5 and 57 per cent alcohol by volume. There are three identifiable classes of vodka products: (1) internationally marketed vodkas mostly of US or UK origin; (2) locally produced vodkas which are generally significantly cheaper; (3) East European vodkas. Ibid.

11. *Revue vinicole internationale*, March 1981.

12. FAO, *Trade Yearbook 1980* (Rome, 1981).

13. *South*, February 1983.

14. *Financial Times*, 21 December 1983.

15. Pekka Sulkunen, 'Production, Consumption and Recent Changes of Consumption of Alcoholic Beverages', *British Journal of Addiction to Alcohol and Other Drugs*, 71 (1976), pp. 3 – 11. Sulkunen observed (in 1976) that most alcohol was consumed domestically, close to raw material sources — only 10 per cent of wine, 2 per cent of beer and 20 per cent of all spirits were exported.

16. Figures from the *Produktschap voor Gedistilleerde Dranken* (Netherlands, 1981).

17. The USA, where comparative data are available for the past 130 years, reveals an interesting fact. While *per capita* alcoholic beverage levels are presently the highest in that 130-year history, at no time except during Prohibition (1920 – 33) and the two years following were they under half their current levels (measured in gallons of pure alcohol). Consumption levels in 1850 were 74 per cent of present levels. See US Department of Health and Human Services, *Fourth Special Report to the US Congress on Alcohol and Health* (Washington DC, January 1981), p. 17.

18. *Le Monde*, 18 April 1982.

19. Whereas approximately one-third of the drinking-age population in the USA

are abstainers, less than 10 per cent of the same group in France abstain. These can be compared with the majority of people reared in Islamic, Hindu and ascetic Protestant traditions who do not drink alcohol. See David Pittman, *Primary Prevention of Alcohol Abuse and Alcoholism: An Evaluation of the Control of Consumption Policy* (Washington University, St Louis, 1980), pp. 6, 33. Since these data measure only legal commercial beverage consumption, they obviously substantially under-report consumption emanating from illicit output and imports.

20. Figures for 14 DEs computed from *Produktschap voor Gedistilleerde Dranken*, (1981). For Zambia, see Muyunda Mwanalushi, 'The African experience', *World Health* (August 1981), p. 14. Part of the increase reflects the substitution of Western commercial beverages for traditional Zambian ones.

21. *World Drinks Report*, 10 December 1980.

22. US personal consumption expenditures on alcohol topped $38.8 billion in 1979, around 2.6 per cent of aggregate expenditures. Calculated from data in US Department of Commerce, *National Income and Product Accounts, 1976 – 1979*, Special Supplement to the Survey of Current Business (Washington DC, July 1981), p. 16.

23. Computed from data in: UK Department of Employment, *Family Expenditure Survey: Report for 1980 giving the results for the United Kingdom* (London, HMSO), 1982.

24. *Time*, 2 April 1979.

25. Still, Germans spend over twice as much on beer as on coffee: DM 16.7 billion versus DM 7.9 billion for coffee (1980). *World Drinks Report*, 28 October 1981. A similar phenomenon is observable in the USA, where alcoholic beverages accounted for only 34.5 per cent of beverage consumption by volume, but for well over half of consumer expenditures on beverages (1980). *Beverage World*, April 1981.

26. Amongst the DMEs, tea is the lending beverage (by volume) only in the UK, where it has a commanding 37 per cent share. *World Drinks Report*, 12 May 1981.

27. *Business Week*, 11 January 1982.

28. *Impact: Marketing, Financial and Economic News and Research for the Wine and Spirits Executive* (henceforth referred to as *Impact*), 1 – 15 January 1979.

29. *Impact*, 15 October 1979.

30. *World Drinks Report*, 4 August 1981.

31. For an explanation of this process in Brazil, see *New Scientist*, 16 July 1981.

32. Illicit output and traffic covers alcoholic beverages produced and sold outside legal marketing channels. It should also be noted that the preceding statistical analysis excluded a certain volume of legally home-brewed distilled spirits, wine, beer, hard ciders, etc., which are seldom systematically recorded by government agencies.

33. *Financial Times*, 29 June 1981.

34. Dr Jonas Boada, 'Rapport sur les problèmes de l'alcool au Venezuela', Caracas, unpublished, 1977.

35. There are also cases of beer smuggling, particularly into countries which have banned beer imports. It is estimated that smuggled imports represent 2 – 3 per cent of total Nigerian beer consumption, but returns are relatively low on this bulk item. *Financial Times*, 3 November 1981. It may be surmised that the figures for more expensive wine and distilled spirits would be higher. To be sure, the extent of contraband trade was estimated at 30 – 50 per cent for certain products (e.g. batteries, cosmetics and textiles). The marketing milieu in which such practices flourish was incisively described by a Nigerian businessman:

Corruption in Nigeria's governmental bureaucracies has been tolerated for so long, it is not likely to be wiped out by an executive order from the President's office or by firing a few high level officials. One must remember that politics and government service in Nigeria are viewed by most people as very lucrative businesses — an easy road to quick money. (*Business Week*, 22 February 1982.)

36. The numbers arrested or fined in 1981 were impressive: 15 wholesalers, 40 companies falsely designated as industrial alcohol producers, 46 producers of blended products and 3 distillers. *Brewing and Distilling International*, February 1982.
37. *International Herald Tribune*, 30 July 1981.
38. Consumer Association of Penang (CAP), *Utusan Konsumer*, August 1981. See also, Dr T. Marimuthu, 'The Illicit Samsu Problem in Malaysia', paper prepared for CAP seminar on Health, Food and Nutrition, 15 – 20 September 1979.
39. *Bottom Line on Alcohol in Society (US)*, Summer 1977 and Spring 1981.
40. *Financial Times*, 15 February 1979.
41. *Brewing and Distilling International*, November 1981.

# 3 EMPLOYMENT AND TECHNOLOGY

A comprehensive overview of the structure of the global market would be incomplete without coming to grips with two other major forces, namely the labour market and changing technology. While governments are concerned with the serious health and economic costs of alcohol use and abuse, their other major consideration is its economic gain. In addition to tax revenues and export earnings, employment generation in alcohol and alcohol-related industries is also a major consideration.[1]

The employment-generating impact of the alcohol industry varies widely between countries. There are, however, enormous statistical difficulties in measuring its employment impact, inasmuch as many distribution outlets market a vast array of consumer goods of which alcohol is only one. Data suggest that more than 10 per cent of France's population gains its livelihood from alcohol and alcohol-related employment. As a sample of selected countries indicates, alcohol-related employment ranges from France at one end of the spectrum to certain countries at the other end where less than 1 per cent of the population is employed in alcohol (Table 3.1). Whereas these numbers provide a static view of employment in the industry, it is mandatory to understand the larger forces which are having an impact on modifying the employment profile. Paramount among these are technological changes inflecting economies of scale, the microprocessor revolution and the momentum of the global economic crisis, with the latter generating certain countervailing tendencies. While the crisis slashes the level of effective demand for all goods, one of its psycho-economic concomitants is that it stimulates alcoholic consumption in certain milieux.

Although basic chemical and industrial processes of alcohol output have not changed appreciably over the past century,[2] new machine applications in certain processes have transformed it into a highly capital-intensive sector. Net output per employee for UK brewing and malting in 1978 was over £16,000, 101 per cent above the UK overall industrial average; spirits distilling was over £22,000, or 186 per cent above.[3] Even the traditional highly labour-intensive wine cultivation sector is slowly being transformed by mechanised grape picking and scientific advances to halt grape disease.

## Table 3.1: Alcohol-related Employment in Selected Countries, 1969 – 80

| Country | Year | Alcohol-related employment (per cent[a]) |
|---|---|---|
| France | 1977 | more than 10 of total population |
| Japan | 1980 | 5, including 1.5% in alcohol production alone |
| Belgium | 1977 | 3.4 |
| Denmark | 1976 | 3.0 of industrial work-force |
| Australia | 1969 | 2.8 |
| USA | 1975 | 2.0 |
| Finland | 1975 | 1.8 of total population |
| UK | 1976 | 1.5 |
| Sri Lanka | 1979 | 0.7 |
| Sweden | 1979 | 0.6 |
| Switzerland | late 1970s | 0.5 of total population in alcohol production alone |
| Sudan | 1978 | 0.4 |
| Poland | 1975 | 0.2 in alcohol production alone |

Note: a. Refers to percentage of work-force, unless otherwise indicated.
Source: Joy Moser (ed.), *National Profiles* (WHO, 1981).

The 1980s are also ushering in major qualitative changes linked to the microprocessor revolution. A 1980 study by the UK National Economic Development Council (NEDC) investigated the revolutionary potential of microelectronics for the automation of the beer industry. Many of these technological innovations have already been applied at the plant level; others are in the engineering pipeline. Such applied capital-intensive technology is by no means confined to the UK, but extends to other developed economies, from whence it will be propagated via subsidiaries, joint ventures and licensing agreements to developing countries.

The UK report identified numerous microprocessor applications in the following seven major beer manufacturing processes: malting, brewing, fermentation, container packaging, warehousing, stock control and distribution.[4] These levels of electronic technology are spreading into distilling, and, as the wine industry becomes more concentrated, it can also be expected that microprocessor applications will extend to this sector as well.

Nowhere, pehaps, has technology's imprimatur on the global market been more starkly voiced than in the words of the UK's Minister for Information Technology:

Britain is a trading nation and heavily dependent on exports of manufactured goods. If we want to remain competitive and maintain and increase our share of both our domestic and world markets we must be up with our competitors in using the most efficient production techniques . . . The choice is stark: automate or liquidate.[5]

Or, in the no less harsh verdict of the *New York Times*: 'Automate, emigrate or evaporate.'[6]

The employment impact of the microprocessor and other new technologies will, in the first stage, lead to major cutbacks of the work-force at the plant level. Guinness, for example, launched a 'Future Competitiveness Plan' towards the end of 1981, involving a five-year capital outlay of $147 million at its central Dublin brewery that would slice its labour force from 2,600 to 1,500.[7] As such technology is diffused, it will lead to a cutback in unit costs, squeezing out smaller producers for whom the cost of such technology is prohibitive.[8] As ever larger volumes of alcohol are sold in supermarkets in several developed countries, labour-cutting innovations such as scanners and electronic cash registers will also indubitably boost unemployment in the alcohol retail sector.

The preceding geo-economic overview is but a prologue for analysing, at far greater depths, the transnational power complexes which have become the overriding determinant in shaping the global market for alcoholic beverages.

## Notes

1. Direct alcohol employment includes workers in breweries, distilleries and wineries. Alcohol-related employment comprises farmers producing raw materials, internal marketing organisations and a vast array of distribution outlets covering a wide spectrum from pubs to restaurants, and from specialised retail shops to supermarkets.
2. Significant among the changes introduced: fermentation and distilling vessels have increased in size, and automatic and semi-automatic valves and pumps have replaced much of the physical labour; other processes have been combined and rationalised and more effective quality control has been devised.
3. C. W. Thurman, 'The Structure and Role of the Alcoholic Drinks Industry', paper presented at conference on 'Economic Aspects of Alcohol Use and Abuse', University of Essex, 12–15 November 1981.
4. Among these, vital innovations could be mentioned: (1) in malting: microprocessor controls for conveying and operating systems, integration of electronic weighing machines, and stock control; (2) in brewing: for raw materials handling and weighing, liquid metering and temperature control for mashing and other operations; (3) in fermentation: techniques for maintaining carbon dioxide pressure, yeast recovery by centrifuge and blending; (4) in container packaging microprocessor

control of packaging lines; (5) in warehousing: applications for invoicing and reordering; (6) in stock control: engineering applications for volume measurement and optimising stock levels; (7) in distribution: improvement in vehicle maintenance, costing and routing. See UK, NEDC, *Microelectronics and the Brewing Industry* (London, 1980).

5. Kenneth Baker, Speech for the International Production, Engineering and Productivity Exhibition, London, 2 March 1982.

6. *New York Times*, 4 March 1982.

7. *World Drinks Report*, 1 September 1981.

8. Kirin, Japan's leading brewer, is spending an unprecedented $195 million on the construction of one new brewery (completed in 1983) with fully computerised production facilities. Kirin, *Annual Report* (1981), p. 4.

# PART TWO: CORPORATE STRUCTURES

# 4 CONTOURS OF GROWTH

## Historical Overview

In both developed and developing economies, the magnitude of geographical concentration in alcoholic beverage output is matched by accelerating corporate concentration. This chapter investigates the oligopolistic and conglomerate movements that are discernible in the beer, wine and distilled spirits sectors. Diagnosis will be centred on the DMEs as the epicentres of transnational conglomerate structures.

In view, however, of the complexity of corporate power relationships related to the internationalisation of output, trade and capital, analytical probings are also directed toward DEs. In most DEs, which are becoming more closely enmeshed into the global economy, the same forces are also at work fuelling concentration. The transformational forces permeating all sectors of the global economy have had a similar impact on the alcoholic beverage industry, as the following overview indicates.

Crucial to an understanding of the global alcoholic beverage industry are the marketing strategies, structures and interactions of the major corporate actors within contemporary capitalism. Just as a drop of water gives a clue into the chemical composition of the sea, the transformational mutations within the alcoholic beverage industry are symptomatic of, although by no means identical with, the perceptible corporate shifts within the global economy. The present stage in capitalism's development is far removed from the earlier competitively atomistic era of specialised single-product firms operating exclusively within narrow markets, whose untrammelled dominance lasted roughly until the 1870s. With the rise of the holding company during that decade,[1] a new legal framework was born which mobilised capital on an unprecedented scale, opening wide the floodgates for horizontal and vertical integration of corporate structures.

The rationale of horizontal integration emanated from technological advances which generated, amongst other things, economies of scale that made it far less profitable to produce in a single plant. Snowballing of capital accumulation surpluses from single factories led to a multiplication of homogeneous single-product plants whose

41

overriding goal was profit maximisation via market aggrandise-ment. Vertical integration marked one more step in the complexity of capital accumulation, involving the technical implementation of more than one stage of the production process by a given firm.

The upsurge of the TNC on a marked scale can be traced back to the two decades preceding the First World War. Corporations based in North America, Western Europe and Japan implanted subsid-iaries in their colonies, which signalled a prodigious extension of horizontal and vertical integration in the quest for (amongst others) raw materials, investment opportunities for surplus capital, markets and cheap labour. This overseas expansion provided the motive force for the further consolidation and integration of the world market under the aegis of the colonial powers in the service of corporate capital. Concomitant with the ascendancy of TNCs was the growth of monopolistic and oligopolistic power within certain key industrial sectors, strikingly so in petroleum (Standard Oil), tobacco (American Tobacco Company and Imperial Tobacco Com-pany), chemicals (I. G. Farben, ICI and Du Pont), and iron and steel (US Steel and Krupp). In Japan, practically the entire industrial structure was oligopolised by the leading Zaibatsus: Mitsui, Mitsubishi and Sumitomo.

Notwithstanding the introduction of antitrust legislation in the USA at the turn of the century, this drive to concentration was not only speeded up in the inter-war years but also ramified into other industrial sectors, for example automobiles, aviation and the elec-trical industry. Another qualitative shift in capital accumulation occurred in the 1960s and 1970s with the rapid ballooning of the industrial conglomerate, that is a firm producing a range of commo-dities in different and unrelated sectors.

The systemic evolution of industry, however, was by no means exceptional. Similar movements were witnessed in agriculture, trad-ing, banking, insurance and retailing. Traditionally pure plantation corporations like United Fruit (now re-baptised United Brands) evolved through stages of increasing vertical integration and ulti-mately conglomeration. Trading companies, whose roots sink into the nineteenth century and beyond, have extended their operations from single- to multi-commodity trading and, in many cases, have further moved into ancillary operations such as banking, insurance, manufacturing, plantations and brokerage operations.

As with trading companies, banking and finance have undergone a dramatic change both in concentration of corporate units and their

geographical location. This was particularly marked in the displace-
ment of the centre of global finance from London to New York after
1918, and the re-emergence of powerful banking groups in Japan
and the FRG from the mid-1950s onwards. Concentration in retailing still remains limited to a handful of countries notably in North
America, Japan and northern Europe. Notwithstanding the momentum of concentration, even in the DMEs, there are striking
variations in the impetus, pace and direction of concentration in all
of these sectors.

In turning to alcoholic beverages to illustrate this transition, what
is perceived is how corporate capital has been able to pull into its
productive and marketing orbit millions of peasants/farmers, large
and small; workers, migrants and domestics; and consumers in
DMEs and DEs. At the company level, these changes are exemplified
in the eclipse of the small regional brewery, the local winery and the
small distillery by large corporations which are international in
scope, producing dozens of different alcoholic drinks and brands.
Whereas distinct companies existed 20 years ago to handle warehousing, bottling, distilling, marketing and distribution, today these
operations are often embodied in one firm.

Corporate expansion takes place via three strategies: expanding
plant capacity; building new plants; and takeovers and mergers. The
desirability of one strategy as opposed to another will vary in
different markets at different times.[2] A corollary of this is the
winnowing out of smaller and medium-sized firms, speeded up in
times of economic recessions. An arsenal of forces has aided this
process, including technological developments, marketing, finance
and advertising, as well as a factor often overlooked: discounts on
bulk purchasing and selling by the larger firms.[3] Recessionary high
interest rates also exercise a punitive effect on smaller wine and
distilled spirits companies who are squeezed in financing their
stocks.

Blurring of demarcations between different alcohol sectors is
perhaps best seen in the USA, where over half of the wine output is
now produced by large corporations whose traditional strength was
distilled spirits.[4] Even more significant, sizeable shares of alcohol
markets are now controlled by conglomerates. These companies are
able to deploy massive financial resources and well-developed
marketing networks in other products to the skilful marketing of
alcohol.

**The Big 27**

By 1980, there were 27 global corporations that produced alcoholic beverages with sales exceeding one billion dollars (Table 4.1). Their corporate headquarters are based in eight DMEs: UK (9), USA (5), Canada (4), Japan (2), the FRG (2), France (2), South Africa (2) and the Netherlands (1). All are conglomerates, almost all produce at least two beverage categories, and most derive an important segment of their revenues abroad. The web of ownership complexities of the big 27 is exemplified by Philip Morris, which owns 22 per cent of Rothman's International of Britain, which in turn owns 71 per cent of Rothman's of Pall Mall of Canada, which in turn owns 50.1 per cent of Carling O'Keefe. Thus, the number two US brewer is linked to the number one South African wine producer, which is hooked up to the number three Canadian brewer. Significant in the constellation of corporate power is that four of the big 27 rank among the world's top 20 food companies,[5] and five are part of larger tobacco-based conglomerates.

As competitive pressures mount, there is a rising need for corporations to extend control of the marketing chain beyond production into trading and retail channels. Hence British brewers, which pioneered control of pubs, are extending such control by the takeover of major hotels and restaurant chains.[6] Such large distillers as Hiram Walker and Distillers Company Limited (DCL) have bought large importing companies which distribute their brands overseas. Such vertical integration strategies contribute to consolidate alcoholic beverage corporations' control over pricing and the complex operations of marketing and distribution.

Lonrho, the sixth largest alcohol TNC, is indicative of the conglomerate dispersal of these firms.[7] In its output and marketing mix, wine, beer and spirits constitute one of 14 major divisions comprising: mining; agriculture and ranching; hotels; motor vehicles; clearing, forwarding, warehousing and cargo; aircraft; textiles; printing and publishing; exporting, confirming and broking; property; department stores; engineering, steel and manufacturing; and pipelines.[8] It operates around 20 breweries in joint ventures with African governments and municipalities, as well as wineries in France and one of Scotland's major whisky distilleries. Reinforcing Lonrho's alcoholic beverage division is its status as a major international trading company, as well as its extensive marketing web in Africa and beyond. Its power as a mega multi-commodity trader was

## Table 4.1:   Alcoholic Beverages: Leading Corporations, 1980

| Corporation | Corporate headquarters | Total sales ($ bn.) | Net profits ($ mn.) | Employees | Alcoholic beverages as per cent of total sales | Per cent of total sales abroad |
|---|---|---|---|---|---|---|
| Philip Morris | USA | 9.8 | 577 | 72,000 | 25.9 | 15.3 |
| Imperial Group | UK | 9.6 | 196 | 127,300 | n.a.[a] | n.a. |
| Rembrandt Group | South Africa | 8.5 | n.a. | n.a. | n.a. | n.a. |
| Grand Metropolitan | UK | 6.2 | 286 | 126,737 | n.a. | n.a. |
| Coca Cola | USA | 6.0 | 422 | 41,000 | n.a. | 44.7 |
| Lonrho | UK | 5.0 | 108 | 140,000 | 5.6 | 34.8 |
| Allied Breweries[b] | UK | 5.0 | 170 | 84,805 | 69.7 | 27.1 |
| Kirin | Japan | 4.1 | 90 | 15,761 | 92.3 | n.a. |
| BSN Gervais Danone | France | 4.0 | 73 | 47,969 | 23.8 | 32.6 |
| Bayerische[c] | FRG | 3.5 | 44 | n.a. | n.a. | n.a. |
| Anheuser-Busch | USA | 3.3 | 172 | 18,040 | 92.0 | n.a. |
| South African Breweries | South Africa | 3.0 | 156 | n.a. | n.a. | n.a. |
| Reemtsma[d] | FRG | 2.8 | −42 | 11,703 | 31.6 | n.a. |
| Suntory | Japan | 2.8 | n.a. | n.a. | n.a. | n.a. |
| Seagram[e] | Canada | 2.6 | 145 | 15,500 | 100.0 | 92.9 |
| National Distillers | USA | 2.1 | 111 | 14,000 | 35.4 | n.a. |
| Bass | UK | 2.0 | 173 | 65,737 | 93.8 | 6.4 |
| Heublein[f] | USA | 2.0 | 84 | 27,100 | 66.1 | 22.0 |
| Hiram Walker | Canada | 2.0 | 205 | 11,700 | n.a. | n.a. |
| Whitbread | UK | 2.0 | 127 | 40,916 | n.a. | n.a. |
| Distillers Co. Ltd. | UK | 2.0 | 312 | 21,300 | n.a. | n.a. |
| Heineken | Netherlands | 1.5 | 39 | 20,532 | 86.4 | n.a. |
| Guinness | UK | 1.4 | 54 | 22,452 | 63.7 | 51.0 |
| Pernod Ricard | France | 1.4 | 58 | 7,200 | n.a. | n.a. |
| Labatt[e] | Canada | 1.3 | 31 | 13,000 | 44.9 | n.a. |
| Molson | Canada | 1.2 | 34 | 12,481 | 46.4 | 56.0 |
| Scottish & Newcastle | UK | 1.1 | 66 | 27,830 | n.a. | n.a. |

Notes: a. Not available.

b. Name changed to Allied-Lyons in 1982.

c. Bayerische Hypotheken- und Wechselbank and Dresdner Bank have part ownership in several FRG breweries.

d. Taken over by coffee-based firm Tchibo in 1981.

e. Figures for Seagram and Labatt are vastly understated, as both are part of large Bronfman holding companies.

f. Taken over by tobacco-based R. J. Reynolds in 1982.

Source: Sales and profit figures from *Business Week* and annual reports; employee figures from *Fortune* and annual reports; other figures from *Forbes* and annual reports.

further extended in 1981 with the acquisition of 50 per cent of Kühne and Nagel, one of the world's biggest cargo, warehousing and forwarding businesses, which pushed Lonrho into 20 new countries.

A more recent entrant into the alcohol corporate elite is American Brands, the oldest US tobacco company which acquired the 190-year-old Jim Beam distilling company. Its portfolio of acquisitions includes the 126-year-old British tobacco company, Gallaher; the 101-year-old cosmetics maker, Andrew Jergens; the 134-year-old private detective company, Pinkerton's; and the 99-year-old Franklin Life Insurance Company. Like other tobacco giants, American Brands is able to inject its tobacco profits into the expansion of its food, alcohol and other activities, as well as the diversification of its product portfolio.

Such concentration at the firm level is reflected in the growing concentration of output in many national markets. In certain countries, like Japan and Brazil, one corporation controls well over half the domestic beer market. In the bulk of developed countries, less than five corporations control over half of the domestic output of beer and distilled spirits,[9] and a similar movement is now coursing through the wine sector.[10]

## Notes

1. The holding company: 'Any company, incorporated or unincorporated, which is in a position to control, or materially to influence, the management of one or more other companies by virtue, in part at least, of its ownership of securities in the other company or companies.' See T. C. Bonbright and G. C. Means, *The Holding Company: Its Public Significance and Its Regulation*, reprint (New York, 1969), p. 10. The state of New Jersey was the birthplace of the modern holding company when, in 1888, it added to its stock corporation law provisions for a corporation articled in the state to include in its charter the specific power to hold stocks in other corporations. The impact of this legislative innovation on the dynamics of capital accumulation was that it entailed economic consequences that have 'seldom been equalled in the entire history of business legislation' (ibid., p. 337).

2. In 1982, according to Stroh's calculations, the cost advantages of a merger, as against building a new factory, were marked: $25 per bbl. of annual productive capacity in merging with Schlitz versus $60 – 80 per bbl. for a new plant. *Time*, 26 April 1982.

3. According to Whitbread's purchasing director, the company records input costs of 4 per cent less than the British industry average through its bulk purchases. *Financial Times*, 14 July 1982.

4. Such a blurring of alcohol categories also occurs internationally. This is witnessed in Whitbread's (UK) $155 million takeover of Nabisco's (US) Julius Wile Sons wine and spirits subsidiary which, in addition to importing and distributing, produces Fleischmann's gin and vodka. *Wall Street Journal*, 27 July 1982.

5. These include Coca Cola (number 9), the Imperial Group (10), Grand Metropolitan (12), and BSN Gervais Danone (19). *L'Expansion*, 6 – 19 November 1981.

6. Among the brewers that control major UK hotel chains are Bass through its control of Crest Hotels (54 hotels); Scottish and Newcastle with Thistle Hotels (39); Allied-Lyons with Embassy Hotels (42); Grand Metropolitan with Comfort Hotels (8); and the Imperial Group/Allied-Lyons with Anchor Hotels (34). Collectively, the big six brewers own hundreds of restaurant outlets. See *Financial Times*, 18 February 1984.

7. An even larger firm of this kind is Unilever, the world's biggest food company, whose subsidiary, United Africa Company, is heavily involved in brewing in both Nigeria and Ghana.

8. Lonrho, *Annual Report*, 1981.

9. Certain sectors with backward linkages to the beer and distilled spirits industries are also highly concentrated. Malting is a prime example, where two companies dominate the world market: the Canadian Malting Company and Associated British Maltsters, the latter a part of the Dalgety Group which is one of the world's top 20 food companies. *Wine and Spirit*, June 1981.

10. It should be understood that TNC market share percentages, in themselves, can understate the extent of power of the leading TNCs in a given sector, an element embodied in the Herfindahl index, which postulates 'that market leaders have even greater economic power in an industry than can be assumed by their market shares' (*Fortune*, 31 May 1982). One facet of this index is that a firm's national market share is often less than its market share in selected local, state or regional markets. One factor that emerged when US brewer Stroh attempted to buy out Schlitz was that, while their combined national market share would only be 13 per cent, that figure would jump as high as a quarter in certain states. *The Economist*, 3 April 1982.

# 5 DYNAMICS OF BEER

Before analysing the historic specificities of corporate market structures in various countries, it is mandatory to underline certain traits common to all. Concentration in the beer industry is more conspicuous than in any other alcoholic beverage sector. Indeed, the only other beverage or liquid sector which approximates its concentration is soft drinks, with Coca Cola and PepsiCo the hegemonic corporate actors. Concentration has been propelled by the swift metamorphosis in output (via expanding economies of scale) and marketing technology. The decade of the 1970s witnessed a revolution in marketing technology led by such conglomerates as Philip Morris, which deployed their highly sophisticated advertising and promotional tactics so successfully tested in tobacco to beer and other industries. This speeded up the winnowing out of brewing companies in many countries, which ineluctably will accelerate in the 1980s (Table 5.1).

Table 5.1: Global Decline of Brewing Companies, 1960 – 80

| Country | Number of companies | | | Index 1960 = 100 | | |
|---|---|---|---|---|---|---|
| | 1960 | 1970 | 1980 | 1960 | 1970 | 1980 |
| Sweden | 57 | 21 | 9 | 100 | 37 | 16 |
| USA | 171 | 92 | 43 | 100 | 54 | 25 |
| UK | 247 | 96 | 81 | 100 | 37 | 33 |
| Finland | 15 | 9 | 5 | 100 | 60 | 33 |
| Netherlands | 38 | 16 | 14 | 100 | 42 | 37 |
| Mexico | 10 | 9 | 5 | 100 | 90 | 50 |
| Italy | 24 | 16 | 12 | 100 | 67 | 50 |
| Portugal | 4 | 4 | 2 | 100 | 100 | 50 |
| Belgium | n.a.[a] | 190 | 100 | n.a. | 100 | 52 |
| France | n.a. | 87 | 50 | n.a. | 100 | 57 |
| Switzerland | 58 | 54 | 33 | 100 | 93 | 57 |
| Norway | 23 | 16 | 14 | 100 | 70 | 61 |
| FRG | 2,180 | 1,750 | 1,364 | 100 | 80 | 63 |
| Australia | 11 | 9 | 7 | 100 | 82 | 64 |
| Austria | 75 | 65 | 51 | 100 | 87 | 68 |
| Denmark | 28 | 23 | 19 | 100 | 82 | 68 |
| Ireland | 6 | 5 | 5 | 100 | 83 | 83 |
| Japan | 4 | 4 | 5 | 100 | 100 | 125 |

Note: a. Not available.
Source: Calculated from data supplied by trade sources.

Single line 'pure' beer companies, outgrowths of the nineteenth century, are dwindling in number. Scrutiny of the top global 30 beer firms reveals that the bulk has overspilled into other beverage sectors, and many of the more aggressively powerful have extended into wholly unrelated activities. Motivations of this compulsive drive to conglomeration, which epitomises the history of Philip Morris, have been lucidly articulated by R. J. Reynolds: 'First, having captured one-third of the United States cigarette market, the company could see a point of diminishing returns for growth potential. Second, significant cash was being generated which could be invested advantageously elswhere.' In adapting what it baptised as 'an unrestricted approach' towards conglomeration, Reynolds shifted into entirely new areas 'on the theory that it made sense, when appropriate, to apply cash to any strong, well-established business'.[1]

Conglomerate thrusts are also transforming the industry's ownership patterns, seen in the partial eclipse of once deeply entrenched family firms. This movement has been accentuated by burgeoning inflation and escalating interest rates, which have pushed costs beyond the capabilities of many family firms' exiguous capital base. In this era of mounting economic concentration,[2] exacerbated by the pervasiveness of the global economic crisis, corporate annexationism is often a pre-condition of growth and survival. Those best equipped to survive are the giant conglomerates, with unequalled and, at times, preferential access to capital markets.

The onslaught of concentration and conglomeration has meshed with a parallel movement. During the twentieth century, a growing number of brewers broke the confines of their regional markets and created brands for the national market. In all DMEs, with the possible exception of the FRG, the scramble for larger market shares is being fought out on national markets. To create effectively national markets, large brewers have set up branch plants at strategic locations to slash transport costs and ensure a more coherent marketing network. More recently, giant companies with sizeable capital resources massively penetrated overseas markets through subsidiaries, joint ventures and licensing arrangements. This augurs further concentration in national beer sectors.

**The Major Groups**

For analytical and expository purposes, the world capitalist beer economy has been subdivided into four major groups. These subdivisions include a sample of countries which produce over two-thirds of the beer brewed globally (including the centrally planned economies).

*Group A* comprises the four leading DME producers which account for 45 per cent of the world's beer output by volume, a figure that excludes a sizeable amount of beer produced through their subsidiaries, joint ventures and licensees in the other three groups and elsewhere.

*Group B* embraces several DMEs where oligopolistic or quasi-monopolistic structures hold sway, but where output and marketing operations of their leading corporations are still largely confined to a national market.

In contrast, *Group C* comprises smaller DMEs where quasi-monopolistic firms have largely overspilled their national markets and driven into the global market.

Finally, *Group D* straddles developing countries where patterns of concentration similar to those of the DMEs are discernible, in several cases under the control of TNCs.

Levels of corporate concentration are indicated in the table accompanying each group. In all cases, with the exception of the FRG, a handful of giant corporations control over half of the national beer output. In South Africa, this concentration attains its apogee with South African Breweries (SAB) appropriating almost 100 per cent of national output.

In view of the beer economy's internationalisation, data of national market shares must be complemented by the international market shares of the major corporations (Table 5.2). Already, the top 30 beer corporations control well over two-fifths of the global beer market, a magnitude which does not include their overseas operations.

**Group A**

Group A comprises countries at four levels of advanced corporate concentration with massive beer markets (Table 5.3). The FRG

Table 5.2: Beer: Global Market Shares[a] by Firm, 1979/80

| Rank | Corporation | Country | Market Share (per cent) |
|---|---|---|---|
| 1 | Anheuser-Busch | USA | 6.48 |
| 2 | Philip Morris (Miller) | USA | 4.83 |
| 3 | Kirin Brewery | Japan | 3.08 |
| 4 | Heineken | Netherlands | 2.84[b] |
| 5 | Brahma | Brazil | 2.01 |
| 6 | Pabst Brewing | USA | 1.91 |
| 7 | Jos. Schlitz Brewing | USA | 1.88 |
| 8 | Adolf Coors | USA | 1.74 |
| 9 | G. Heileman | USA | 1.69 |
| 10 | Bass | UK | 1.53 |
| 11 | BSN Gervais Danone | France | 1.35 |
| 12 | United Breweries | Denmark | 1.34 |
| 13 | Cerveceria Modelo | Mexico | 1.09 |
| 14 | Allied-Lyons | UK | 1.01 |
| 15 | Sapporo | Japan | 0.98 |
| 16 | Whitbread | UK | 0.96 |
| 17 | South African Breweries | South Africa | 0.93 |
| 18 | Cerveceria Cuauhtemoc | Mexico | 0.90 |
| 19 | Grand Metropolitan (Watney Mann) | UK | 0.88 |
| 20 | Cerveceria Moctezuma | Mexico | 0.84 |
| 21 | Molson | Canada | 0.82 |
| 22 | Scottish and Newcastle | UK | 0.79 |
| 23 | Stroh Brewing | USA | 0.79 |
| 24 | San Miguel | Philippines | 0.78 |
| 25 | Olympia | USA | 0.78 |
| 26 | Brascan (Labatt) | Canada | 0.78 |
| 27 | DUB Schultheiss | FRG | 0.77 |
| 28 | Tchibo (Reemtsma) | FRG | 0.77 |
| 29 | Oetker | FRG | 0.71 |
| 30 | Imperial Group (Courage) | UK | 0.62 |
| | Others | | 54.12 |
| | World total | | 100.00 |

Notes: a. Market shares computed on basis of brewer's own output as per cent of world commercial beer output; excludes firms' overseas output.

b. Includes output of overseas subsidiaries, joint ventures and licensees. If only Dutch output computed, Heineken would rank 26.

Source: Computed from data supplied by UK Brewers Society and trade sources.

represents an early stage of oligopoly, where three well-positioned, medium-sized companies stand poised for continued market aggrandisement. A further concentration stage is witnessed in the UK, where an oligopoly of six firms (to which might be added Guinness) is rapidly impinging on regional brewers' markets. Anheuser-Busch and Philip Morris's duopolistic control of the US market presents yet a higher stage, surpassed in Group A only by Kirin's quasi-monopolistic grip on the Japanese market. The bulk of the corporate leaders in all four are conglomerates, which already overflow the confines of vast indigenous consumer markets.

## The USA

From 1623, when the first commercial brewery was set up in New Amsterdam, the USA has grown into the world's leading beer producer, with almost a quarter of global output at present. Growth of the beer sector, as in several other industrial sectors, traversed two historic phases: a proliferation of small-scale, labour-intensive competitive breweries that prevailed roughly up to the end of the nineteenth century; sequelled by rapid concentration after the Second World War. Numbers of companies plummeted from 1,700 in the pre-prohibition era to 750 in 1935, to 150 in 1962 and to 43 at present.[3]

Table 5.3:    Concentration in the Beer Industry, 1979/80, Group A

| Country | Country rank in global beer sales | Leading corporations | Corporation rank in global beer sales | Per cent of national market | |
|---|---|---|---|---|---|
| USA | 1 | Anheuser-Busch | 1 | 28.7 | |
| | | Philip Morris | 2 | 21.9 | |
| | | Pabst | 6 | 8.6 | 75.4 |
| | | Schlitz | 7 | 8.4 | |
| | | Coors | 8 | 7.8 | |
| FRG | 2 | DUB Schultheiss | 27 | 7.6 | |
| | | Tchibo | 28 | 7.6 | 22.2 |
| | | Oetker | 29 | 7.0 | |
| UK | 4 | Bass | 10 | 21.5 | |
| | | Allied-Lyons | 14 | 14.0 | |
| | | Whitbread | 16 | 13.5 | 79.6 |
| | | Grand Metropolitan | 19 | 12.4 | |
| | | Scottish & Newcastle | 22 | 10.3 | |
| | | Imperial | 30 | 7.9 | |
| Japan | 5 | Kirin | 3 | 63.0 | |
| | | Sapporo | 15 | 20.0 | 95.0 |
| | | Asahi | 31 | 12.0 | |

Source: Data computed from corporation annual reports and trade sources.

The present number of brewers is, however, singularly misleading since the top six accounted for over four-fifths of output in 1980, as against less than two-fifths in 1960 (Figure 5.1). By 1981, the top

Figure 5.1: USA: Market Shares of Six Largest Brewers, 1951–81

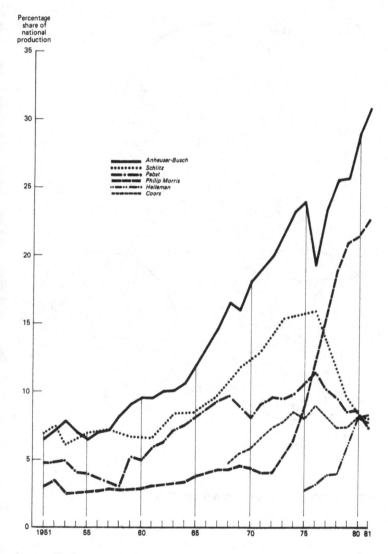

Source: Trade sources.

Figure 5.2:  US Beer: Corporate Profile, 1961 – 81

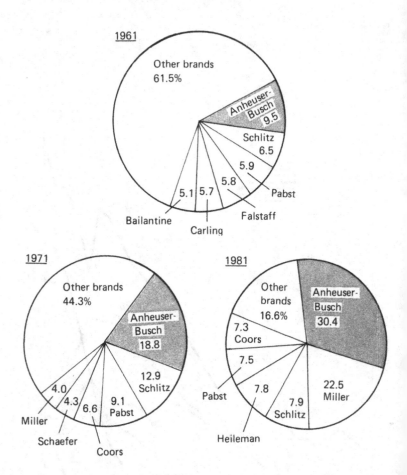

Source: *Modern Brewery Age* (various issues, 1983).

two — Anheuser-Busch and Philip Morris (through its subsidiary Miller Beer) — had appropriated more than half the US market, thus dramatically widening the gap between them and the remaining four (each with around 8 per cent of the market). That same year, the top six recorded 83 per cent of US sales, while the remaining 37 companies scrambled for the other 17 per cent (Figure 5.2). The immense size of the US beer market, now outstripping $16.5 billion, is of the same order of magnitude as that of cigarettes and soft drinks. Dominance of the major beer corporations is seen in their ranking amongst the top beverage corporations in the USA. Of the twelve largest US beverage corporations (ranked by 1980 beverage sales), seven are principally beer companies.[4]

*Configuration of Concentration.* There are several determinants behind the push to concentration. As in many industries, growth has been fostered by successive merger waves which have not been appreciably halted by antitrust legislation. Between 1958 and 1975, at least 88 beer plants or brands were taken over and merged into others. Quite often, acquisitions not only entailed the purchase of another company, but also included brands and distributorships.

Also of pivotal importance have been the colossal strides in economies of scale at the plant level (i.e. minimum efficient plant size) over the past two decades, which have driven hundreds of small brewers into insolvency. By the mid-1960s, the majors began erecting breweries that were often more than double the capacity of previous plants. This was facilitated by engineering breakthroughs, which halved labour costs.[5] The significance of these sharply rising scale economies is seen in the shifting minimum efficient size of a single plant: from about 1 million barrels yearly in 1960, to roughly 2 million in 1970, doubling once again to around 4 million in 1978.[6] Since the late 1970s, the inception of computerised production lines has further escalated scale economies to a point where Philip Morris is now building a 10 million barrel brewery, which could well be a pace-setter for the industry in the latter half of the 1980s.

Another impetus to concentration is oligopolistic pricing policies by the majors, at times including pricing below costs to acquire larger market shares. Such marketing strategies, spawning brand loyalties rooted in product differentiation and market segmentation, are ideally adopted to the operations of a large conglomerate but, once again, are outside the cost capabilities of the smaller firm.

Uninhibited advertising and promotional outlays have also

become one of the major factors abetting the tempo of concentration. Inexorably, this has led to a shift in the industry as marketing, predicated on multi-million dollar advertising onslaughts, matched production technology as an effective instrument of corporate warfare.

During the late 1970s, the combined impact of double-digit inflation and high interest rates further undermined smaller firms. Certain characteristics of large corporations partially insulate them from these twin battering rams, notably vertical integration which extends from control of the raw material phases up to final distribution. Because of this integrated control over vast areas of output and marketing processes, a mega corporation is positioned to set internal transfer prices to mitigate the buffetings of inflation. Moreover, purchases usually involve such large volumes that far higher discounts can be extracted from external suppliers than those negotiated by smaller firms.

*Case Histories.* In 1969, one of the world's leading tobacco corporations, Philip Morris, acquired a 53 per cent stake in the number seven brewer Miller,[7] an advance consolidated a year later by the appropriation of the remaining stocks. The newcomer's corporate profile was, in all respects, different from previous entrants: already in 1970 its total sales scaled $1 billion; it was a leader in tobacco, trailing only R. J. Reynolds; and it produced over 100 cigarette brands in over 100 countries through a highly honed national and international distribution network[8].

Philip Morris's marketing prowess owed much to its skilful transferral of techniques that catapulted it from number six to number two in the US tobacco industry, pithily summarised by *Business Week* in the mid-1970s: 'The approach calls for dividing up the US beer market into demand segments, producing new products and packages specifically for those segments, and then spending with abandon to promote them.'[9] Such spending 'with abandon' led to Philip Morris's beer advertising outlays leaping by 387 per cent (1971 – 8) compared to 236, 160 and 175 per cent for its three major competitors.[10] While the Miller subsidiary's advertising budget soared from $11 million to $75 million between 1972 and 1979, its market share shot up from 4 per cent to over 22 per cent.[11]

Major changes were wrought in the US beer industry as a result of Philip Morris's conglomerate strategies and structures. How was it possible, it could be asked, for a corporation to pursue both massive plant expansion and unprecedented advertising onslaughts without incurring large losses? Indeed, Philip Morris's Miller subsidiary did sustain substantial deliberate losses.[12] Part of its beer subsidiary's expansion was financed by access to capital markets, as Philip Morris boosted its total debt by over a billion dollars (1971 – 7). As one of its embittered competitors lamented: 'It is definitely taking profits from one business and sticking them into another business to gain market share below cost.'[13]

Nor was Philip Morris's Miller compelled to make any return on its invested capital in the short term. Or, as one corporate analyst commented: 'The thing that all the other brewers have in common is that they have to make a decent return on investment; for now that is not the case with Miller.'[14] Such is the privileged climate of conglomeration.

Already by the mid-1970s, however, the pay-off had commenced when, in 1976, Miller's net income wiped out all of Philip Morris's earlier losses on beer. This triumph of cross-subsidisation led the Chairman of Philip Morris's beer subsidiary to declare:

> Although we can be proud, we are not content. We did not come into the beer business to become number four. We have one simple objective — to be number one. That's what we are after, and that's what we'll do . . .[15]

Theoretically, such annexationist strides and strivings are explicable in the context of a conglomerate's role in an oligopolistic sector, illuminated by John Blair, one of the leading theorists of economic concentration:

> . . . in the forms of rivalry to which oligopolists typically limit themselves, i.e. advertising, sales effort, services and other types of non-price competition, the advantages tend to go to the firm with the greatest resources, not the lowest costs. Hence, the conglomerate, because of its greater resources, may be expected to improve its position over time at the expense of the other oligopolists. Ultimately, the strength of the latter may be so reduced as to render them unable to pursue an independent course of conduct, even when they are so inclined.[16]

Expanding this line of argument, Blair went on to note that certain industries are particularly susceptible to conglomerate intrusions:

'The danger of competition posed by cross-subsidization, whether actual or anticipated, is at a maximum in unconcentrated industries populated largely by single-line firms.'[17] This theoretical model clearly depicts the parameters of the US beer industry at the time of the Philip Morris onslaught.

In less than a decade after Philip Morris's annexation, the industry had been transformed from a fairly loose oligopoly of single-line firms into what might be portrayed as a duopoly, led by two conglomerates: Anheuser-Busch and Philip Morris. Anheuser-Busch stands isolated in the US beer industry in its ability, thus far, to match the financial and marketing power of PM, and hence was the only other firm to raise massively its market share during the 1970s.

In the economic war for bigger market shares, Anheuser-Busch has retained its hegemony on global beer markets through three interlocking strategies: vertical integration, conglomeration and internationalisation. Vertical integration is characterised by linkages backwards into raw materials and forwards into distribution. This envelops such activities as processing barley into brewer's malt, production of baker's yeast (in which it is the nation's leading producer), manufacture of metal containers (producing 311 billion beer cans in 1980), rice handling and storage facilities, a trucking fleet, a railway company and a metallised label printing operation.

Its thrust into conglomeration, while far less pronounced than that of Philip Morris, is nonetheless conspicuous. This has been spearheaded by extensions into the family entertainment business, real estate development, a major league baseball team, a soft drink division and a wide variety of snack foods. In several of these product lines it has effectively mobilised its extensive marketing and distribution network first tested and developed in beer.

Its most recent conglomerate takeover was the $570 million merger with the country's second largest wholesale cake baking and bread business, Campbell Taggart (1981 sales: $1.7 billion). As well as operating in Spain, France and Brazil, Campbell Taggart runs 63 plants in the USA, and a restaurant chain of 92 outlets with alcoholic beverage licenses. In addition to these allurements, it was considered operationally complementary by Anheuser-Busch as both are capital-intensive, require plants to operate at high capacity levels, and are endowed with complex transport and distribution networks. In addition, Anheuser-Busch's yeast operations feed directly into the baking plants of its new subsidiary.

The creation of Anheuser-Busch International, a licensing and marketing subsidiary formed to explore and develop markets outside the USA, is yet a further development in the quest for larger market shares. Already it has forged links with a major Canadian brewery, Labatt,[18] that brews and distributes Anheuser-Busch's leading brand Budweiser in Canada.

In contrast to the expansionary drive of the two giant conglomerates, the middle tier of four medium-sized companies (Schlitz, Pabst, Coors and Heileman) are battling for survival. The gap in market shares between these four, each with about 8 per cent of the market, and the big two should continue to widen, given the continuous disparities in cash flows available for marketing offensives. Survival in the medium and long term is contingent upon their ability to merge. Already by 1982, Stroh (number seven) and Schlitz (number three) agreed to merge, Pabst (number five) was taking over Olympia (number eight), and Heileman (number four) and Schmidt (number ten) were aggressively seeking acquisitions. As Heileman's chairman put it: 'It's inevitable that if we are to preserve an effective, competitive second tier, you've got to let those companies combine. Either those things will happen or they will disappear.[19] One of the paradoxes of antitrust legislation is that one of the few major rulings in recent years barring a merger was in the beer industry, precisely to block the competing efforts by Heileman and Pabst to annex Schlitz. Antitrust, in this specific case, could very well reinforce the duopoly's further advance, inasmuch as it perpetuates the relative fragmentation of their competitors.

## The UK

The UK's beer economy presents yet another variation of concentrated economic power. Whereas the USA is becoming a classic example of a beer duopoly, the UK indicates a somewhat more distinct case of oligopoly, with the big six dividing four-fifths of the national market. Seven regional firms plus 65 'independent' companies share the rest of the market. Roots of this concentration reach back into the middle of the eighteenth century when excise returns revealed that a dozen big London breweries accounted for about a quarter of national output. Such pre-industrial manifestations of concentration, when thousands of breweries were entirely localised, were very different from those of the post-1880 era.

At the onset of the twentieth century, there were nearly 1,500 independent brewers operating around 6,500 separate breweries. By 1937, their numbers had been whittled down to 1,000, which was speeded up in successive decades with around 80 companies operating some 160 breweries in 1982. The intensification of the economic crisis and stagnation of beer consumption in 1983 contributed to a rapid speed up of concentration: 14 of the small independent brewers closed shop.

Historically, a salient feature of the largest UK brewers that differentiates them from their DME counterparts is their unique inter-connections with the retailing network. Pubs remain the central retail outlet in the UK. Their ownership is dominated by the big six and much of their promotional efforts are carried out through these pubs. This dissimilarity with the USA, however, is matched by a similarity, since half of the big six have either been appropriated by conglomerates, or have launched their own conglomerate extensions. Epitomising this drive to conglomeration are the giant firms: Imperial Group, Grand Metropolitan and Allied-Lyons.

The big six's inevitable expansion will further alter the power constellation of the 60 – 65 smaller 'independent' brewers, each with less than 1 per cent of the national market. There are certain factors which have contributed to the survival of the smaller companies, including higher rates of return on capital in both production and wholesaling. Big boosts in fuel prices since 1973 have shot up the big six's distribution costs, while the smaller breweries minimise fuel costs by concentrating supplies to outlets within a 30-mile radius of their plants.[20] Also, the popular campaign for real ale (unpasteurised beer), which has promoted local brands and loyalties, has been another contributory factor. But these are at best short-term holding operations, since much larger forces are at work that will circumvent and vitiate these advantages.

Among these larger forces are technological innovations that will slash unit costs, in turn fuelling higher productivity and rates of return on investment. In recessionary periods, when the industry is operating well below the 75 – 80 per cent rate that is considered a profitable threshold, only the bigger brewers have the financial staying power to ride out the storm. Whereas the big six are all publicly-owned corporations (i.e. a corporation whose shares are bought and sold on the stock market), 47 of the smaller breweries are believed to be family controlled, and family influence is considerable in others. These ownership patterns limit the smaller brewers' access to financial resources and thus their capability to survive recession.[21] In a larger sectoral context, this indicates that sustained global economic crises exercise a highly differential impact on different sized firms. It is precisely during cyclical downswings that the absorption of smaller firms is speeded up.

While a distinction is often made between the big six and the 60 – 65 so-called 'independent' brewers (occasionally referred to as regionals), in reality such differentiation can be misleading. Closer scrutiny of the ownership structure of two of the so-called 'independents' that merged in 1982 (Boddingtons and Oldham) unveils that certain of the big six owned large volumes of shares in both. Whitbread owned 26 per cent of Boddingtons and both Whitbread and Allied-Lyons owned 10 per cent each of Oldham. What role the big two played in consummating the merger is not public knowledge. From fragmentary indicators, however, a partial picture of the big six's ownership penetration of the so-called independents emerges: 17 are partially or wholly owned by one or more of the big six, with three others owned by non-beer TNCs.[22] Such intricate ownership patterns are also dissimulated in both developed and developing countries and call for closer investigatory analysis.

*Retail Linkages.* More than in any other country, the UK's big six exercise a preponderant control over the entire beer industry. One of the clues to understanding the scope of this control is their unquestioned dominance over retailing. UK beer retailing has three major outlets: pubs and hotels (which distribute and market around three-fifths), clubs and restaurants, and the 'take-home trade' (or 'off licence'), dominated by the large supermarket chains.[23] The traditionally paramount pub sector can be further subdivided into what are called tied pubs (or tied estates) controlled by brewers, and untied pubs (sometimes referred to jointly with clubs as the 'free trade'). Presently, the big six own roughly half of the UK's 74,000 public houses. Indeed, the extent of control could be very much higher through the big six's ownership of smaller brewers, as the Boddington/Oldham case history reveals.

The sheer marketing value of these tied pubs is that they sell almost exclusively the brands of their brewer owner. The importance that brewers place on this retail linkage is glimpsed in the large-scale investments that they allocate to these outlets. Out of a £459 million UK brewers' investment outlay in 1980, a full 60 per cent was allocated to retailing (particularly pubs), climbing to 67 per cent in 1981.[24] With the deepening of the crisis and stagnating consumption, the share of new capital investment (1983 – 5) in pubs and other retail outlets was projected to rise to 85 per cent of all new investment. This strategy is aimed at capturing consumers from corporate competitors rather than through the build up of new productive capacity.

Extensive corporate control over pubs is obviously not viewed by the big six as enough, hence the retailing offensive to corral the remaining two-fifths of the retail market: primarily the clubs and the take-home trade. The big six have commenced economic war by offering registered clubs easy credit terms, as seen in certain recent Bass loans with repayment up to ten years at zero interest rates. Given current levels of inflation, this is tantamount to a major subsidy which not merely forges closer long-term commercial links, but subordinates these clubs to the corporate imperatives of the big six. The sheer dimensions of subsidised hand-outs by the industry at the end of 1980 amounted to about £300 million to the so-called free trade.

The third retail outlet, the take-home trade, is the fastest growing as large retailers such as Sainsbury and Marks & Spencer have become major alcohol distributors. To dominate more effectively supermarket shelf space, big brewers have launched price wars through such familiar techniques as price discounting, a tested marketing weapon wielded by large corporations in all economic sectors. These marketing assaults, used on all three retailing fronts, are aimed at increasing market shares and are clearly beyond the financial grasp of smaller brewers. Retailing link-ups, as a redoubtable weapon of economic warfare, are thus part of the arsenal of entrenched economic power.

As the global economic crisis deepened in the early 1980s, smaller economic units at both the output and retail level were disappearing. With soaring pub overhead costs and fierce competition from supermarkets, the big six allocated vast capital investments to their tied pubs to boost turnover by developing new services, notably food. In much the same manner, the crisis-induced drop in UK beer sales has engendered a marketing war between brewers to hold on to pub, club and supermarket outlets, with the smaller producer the inevitable victim.

*Conglomerate Extensions.* Conglomeration in the 1960s became a strategy to consolidate corporate growth, augment cash flows and immunise the corporation from the cyclical buffetings of a single product line. Not only did certain UK breweries become the practitioners of such strategies, but also certain large corporations outside the beer industry surged into brewing as a profitable source for conglomerate extension. The first logical marketing step of such extensions for brewers was into other beverage sectors. By 1980, three of the big six brewers derived an important segment of their profits from wine and spirits: Allied-Lyons (40 per cent), Grand Metropolitan (20 per cent) and Whitbread (11 per cent).[25] While traditionally such aggrandisements have involved large corporations acquiring smaller ones, there is a perceptible increase in large corporations annexing divisions of other large corporations. A prominent example is Allied-Lyons' takeover of the wine and spirit interests of Booker McConnell, one of the world's biggest agribusiness enterprises.

Soft drinks represent another profitable area for aggrandisement and certain of the big six, erstwhile competitors in the beer market, are actively collaborating in the sector. Bass and Whitbread merged their soft drinks interests in 1980 to form a joint company, Canada Dry Rawlings, which controls about 6 per cent of the UK soft drink market. Bass is an illustrious example of a company which has reached a first stage of conglomeration, but has yet to overspill the boundaries of the beverage industry. Already it is vertically integrated backwards into malt and forwards into pubs and hotels; and is deeply entrenched in soft drinks, wine and spirits.

A more mature phase of conglomeration is revealed by Allied-Lyons, which has extensions well beyond beer, wine, spirits, soft drinks, tea and coffee, into cakes and confectionery, biscuits, ice cream, food mixes and meat products. Grand Metropolitan and Imperial, ranking among the top ten UK corporations, are the two major conglomerate intruders into the UK brewing industry. As with other tobacco conglomerates, Imperial has swiftly diversified into food and beverages. Its largest acquisition, before the $629 million takeover of the US Howard Johnson restaurant chain in 1980, was its 1972 takeover of the UK Courage Brewing Group. Courage, from its birth in 1787, grew into one of the big six UK brewers with an extensive hotel chain as well as backward and forward linkages into hops, malt, bottling and pubs.[26]

While Imperial continues to generate over half of its revenue from tobacco, it has sizeable extensions in food and food retailing (30 per cent of 1980 assets), as well as paper and plastics to underpin its brewing operations. Imperial's conglomerate extensions are partially glimpsed in Figure 5.3 which depicts the major companies within its five principal groups.

Tobacco's once dominant share has been eroded, as the conglomerate has offset decelerated growth in tobacco consumption by increasing its marketing forays into food and brewing. As with Philip Morris, the Imperial Group has found it highly profitable to transfer almost identical marketing techniques from one addictive commodity to another.

Internationalisation of output and trade has been another feature of the big six's quest to enlarge markets and spheres of marketing influence. None of the major brewers exports more than 2 per cent of its total sales. Rather, internationalisation has been pursued largely via the setting up of subsidiaries and joint ventures overseas. Allied-Lyons has moved furthest in this direction; its overseas output accounted for around a quarter of aggregate sales in 1980.[27]

In the early 1980s, the big six have responded to a stagnant UK beer market[28] with closures and cutbacks, technological innovations, and strategies to slash costs (particularly labour costs). This acquires a new context as labour militancy rises in the UK and it is by no means fortuitous that the big six's three largest closures or cutbacks in 1980 occurred in plants with poor labour relations.[29]

## The FRG

What stands out in the world's second largest beer-producing country is that it remains the only major DME where a handful of firms do not produce over half of the national alcohol output. Indeed, just under half the world's approximately 3,000 breweries are located in that country, ranging in size from very small breweries to a leading group which, by developed countries' standards, would be ranked as medium-sized companies. Four medium-sized companies brew 34 per cent of the FRG's beer (1979), led by DUB Schultheiss (a subsidiary of Bayerische and Dresdner Banks), Tchibo (through its subsidiary Reemtsma) and Oetker.[30] Beer exports are even more highly concentrated, with three brewing groups (Beck, Holsten and Löwenbräu) having three-fifths.[31]

An indicator of the relative smallness of FRG breweries is that by the late 1970s their average annual output of 1.7 million US gallons was massively eclipsed by the US average of 55.5 million. This stems from plant size differentials as well as lower productivity rates in the FRG due to lower levels of capitalisation: each FRG brewery employee produces only about a quarter of his American counter-

## Figure 5.3:  The Imperial Group, 1981

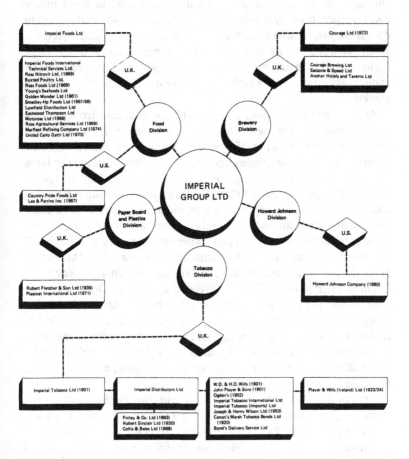

Source:  Imperial Group, Annual Report, 1981.

part. This relative fragmentation, where no German brewer is amongst the world's top 25, finds its counterpart in other major FRG sectors, notably textiles. Persistence of such structures stem in part from historically deeply entrenched regional loyalties. Regionalism, however, as an economic force is not immune to the large national and international corporate strategies and the pressures of capital accumulation which are transforming the US and UK markets.

At the turn of the 1980s, 43 regional brewers accounted for over a third of output. Over the last two decades, however, there has been a noticeable shift in ownership patterns away from exclusive family control. As these companies became public corporations, the large German banks were among the major buyers of their shares. A statistical enquiry into the 133 breweries in the FRG's top 9,500 companies reveals, however, that still as much as 64 per cent of these leading breweries are mainly family-owned, with banks and investment companies being the largest owners of over a quarter of them.[32] By the onset of the 1970s, one bank alone, the Bayerische Hypotheken- und Wechselbank, controlled as much as 17 per cent of German beer output. Today, Bayerische and the Dresdner Bank each own 25 per cent of Germany's largest brewer, DUB Schultheiss. Thus, to designate the market as fragmented is, as with the UK regionals, somewhat misleading, since ownership patterns are often much more concentrated. As in other countries, such complex ownership patterns are concealed by private companies and seldom revealed by public corporations.

Concomitant with the changing configuration of the regionals has been conglomerate movements amongst the largest FRG breweries. DUB, for example, has extended its interests into 42 firms producing several product lines. Most successful are its soft drinks and bottled water units, and more recently it has cross-subsidised declining beer sales with its profits in these two areas. But conglomerates themselves are not immune to conglomerate takeovers. The giant coffee-based family-owned firm of Tchibo acquired (in 1980) 60 per cent of the FRG's number two brewer, Reemtsma. The latter was, however, itself a conglomerate of the species of Imperial and Philip Morris, that is a giant international tobacco-based company with sizeable brewing interests. Even prior to the Tchibo takeover, Reemtsma's cigarette and beverages division had over one hundred subsidiaries and associated companies which girdled the world. Thus, coffee and beer, the two leading beverages in the FRG, are becoming more closely meshed from a corporate perspective.

Although, in an earlier era, Germany was the pace-setter in the internationalisation of breweries, in recent times they have been partially squeezed out of foreign markets by the more aggressive marketing forays of certain of their European and North American competitors. A leading FRG exporter, Löwenbräu, stopped shipping beer to the USA in 1978 and instead sold a licence to Philip Morris to produce and market its product. As the beer industry becomes increasingly concentrated and internationalised, it remains conjectural whether the FRG beer industry will be able to consolidate its hold on the global market, or whether its relative fragmentation will become a deterrent in so doing. In either case, scores of small and medium-sized brewers will be either taken over or liquidated. Munich brewing analysts predict that a quarter of FRG brewers could disappear by 1990.[33] Indeed, this figure could well be surpassed before the decade's end.

## Japan

Unlike the duopolistic US market and various stages of oligopoly in the UK and FRG, the Japanese beer industry might be designated as quasi-monopolistic. Kirin Brewery, the world's third largest brewer (1980 sales: $4.1 billion) controls over 60 per cent of the domestic Japanese market. Its history is inextricably imbricated with the foundations of the beer industry in Japan. It is the corporate descendant of the first brewery set up in 1869 at the birth of the Meiji restoration. From its inception, the industry, like much of Japanese industry and finance, became rapidly concentrated under the corporate umbrella of the Dai Nippon Company.

Although the modern Kirin company was born in 1907, it only acquired market pre-eminence in the early 1960s, aided by the post-war breakup of the historic leader, Dai Nippon. The latter's successor firms, Sapporo and Asahi Breweries, have remained numbers two and three in the industry. Asahi is a particularly potent force on global markets since the corporation is not only a conglomerate in its own right, but is part of one of the world's largest conglomerate groupings: Sumitomo. Jointly with Kirin, the trio controls over 90 per cent of the domestic market. Although Japanese beer sales stagnated in 1980, the trio's technological and market power was such that all reported a rise in profits. Once again, this indicates the operational capability of large corporations (under certain conditions) to ride out cyclical troughs and even to profit by them.

Several novel forces have now begun to exercise a major impact on the industry. Paramount amongst these is the intrusion of Japan's quasi-monopolistic whisky producers, Suntory (1981 sales: $3.5 billion), into the beer market. Kirin, in turn, penetrated Suntory's domain by setting up a joint subsidiary with Seagram in 1972 to produce whisky, gin and vodka. In the corporate battle of the giants, the relatively smaller firms are the most likely to suffer market share losses, thereby reinforcing the quasi-monopolistic strength of Kirin and Suntory.[34] Another factor, in contrast to the USA, has been state intervention aimed at consolidating Kirin's market position, as is evidenced in the 1977 revision of the anti-monopoly law that opened unlimited expansionist horizons.[35] Loosening of the anti-monopoly law is but one example of the Japanese state's historic role of furthering concentration and rationalisation to boost export capacity, with the Ministry of International Trade and Industry (MITI) as the major catalyst.

Kirin, and to a lesser extent Asahi and Sapporo, have continued to expand into all alcoholic and non-alcoholic beverages. As it has largely outgrown the national market, Kirin now directs its marketing energies to the global market, as seen in its spate of recent takeovers, including a US beverage importer, an Australian malt supplier, three Coca Cola bottlers and a Brazilian sake producer. The self-reinforcing nature of certain of these linkages is glimpsed in Kirin's 1982 agreement with Banyu Pharmaceuticals involving biotechnology development, drug manufacturing and sales. In this deal, Kirin benefits from Banyu's antibiotic technologies and sales network, and Banyu, in turn, exploits Kirin's fermentation technology.

Relative fragmentation in the nation's wholesaling and retailing sectors offers another important avenue for profit maximisation by the highly concentrated beer sector. Kirin is able to select its distributors from among a vast spectrum of more than 2,000 wholesalers. There are few, if any, beer wholesalers with enough bargaining power to withstand the margin demand pressures of Kirin. Compared with the other Group A countries that have built up relatively concentrated wholesale/retail sectors, an anomalous situation prevails in Japan where the producers are positioned to squeeze the distributors, instead of vice versa.

What differentiates the big four countries in Group A from other DMEs is their geo-corporate ubiquity in the global beer economy. Nonetheless, the same major corporate drives towards oligopoly, conglomeration and internationalisation are discernible in the other two DME groupings.

## Group B

Group B embraces eight DMEs where convergent corporate market structures are emerging that could be considered as an embryonic stage of development towards Group A. Jointly, these eight produce an eighth of the world's beer, slightly over half the US total. Specific modes of corporate organisation characterising these eight countries are also perceived in certain smaller DMEs not analysed in this book.

Table 5.4 attempts to depict their salient market characteristics. All three sectoral stages of concentration seen in Group A are manifested at varying levels of intensity in Group B. BSN Gervais Danone (51 per cent) in France, and Lion Breweries (55 per cent) in New Zealand correspond, to a lesser extent, to Kirin's quasi-monopolistic dominance in the Japanese market. In Canada, Australia, Belgium, Austria and Switzerland, duopolistic structures akin to those in the USA are being consolidated. Only in Canada and Belgium do large companies exist which could challenge the clear market leadership of the big two. Finally, Spain's market structure is clearly oligopolistic and exhibits traits similar to the UK market.

Already, vertical integration is a feature of Group B's major corporations, followed by a leap into conglomeration by the leading corporations in three countries: France, Canada and Australia. BSN Gervais Danone is one of the world's biggest food corporations. Likewise in Canada, the big three are conglomerate and one of them, Brascan (a Bronfman holding company), has a partially owned (42 per cent) brewing subsidiary, John Labatt, which is itself a multi-divisional conglomerate. In 1982, Labatt moved into first place in the Canadian beer sector, conferring on the Bronfman empire top market position in both distilled spirits and beer.[36]

Australia's big two are highly diversified food producers and are numbered among the largest hotel chain owners in the country. In the largest takeover in Australia's history ($436 million), number one brewer Carlton and United Breweries (CUB) was absorbed by another conglomerate, Elders IXL, which has extensive pastoral, finance, food and other operations in Australia and abroad.

## Table 5.4: Concentration in the Beer Industry, 1979/80, Group B

| Country | Country rank in global beer sales | Leading corporations | Corporation rank in global beer sales | Per cent of national market | Market characteristics |
|---|---|---|---|---|---|
| France | 10 | BSN Gervais Danone | 11 | 51.1 | quasi-monopoly largest firm in conglomerate largest firm inter-nationalised |
| Canada | 11 | Molsons | 21 | 38.2 ⎫ | duopoly (with strong number 3) |
| | | Brascan | 26 | 36.2 ⎬ 97.6 | big 3 all conglomerates |
| | | Carling O'Keefe[a] | — | 23.2 ⎭ | big 3 have strong presence in US market |
| Spain | 12 | El Aguila | — | 21.1 ⎫ | |
| | | Mahon[b] | — | 11.7 ⎪ | oligopoly |
| | | Damon | — | 11.2 ⎬ 63.9 | foreign capital |
| | | San Miguel[c] | — | 10.6 ⎪ | involvement |
| | | Cruz del Campo[d] | — | 9.3 ⎭ | |
| Australia | 13 | Carlton and United Breweries | — | 50.0 ⎫ 80.0 | duopoly |
| | | Castlemaine | | | big 2 are |
| | | Tooheys | — | 30.0 ⎭ | conglomerates |
| Belgium | 15 | Stella Artois | — | 33.0 ⎫ | duopoly |
| | | Piedboeuf[e] | — | 30.2 ⎬ 76.6 | foreign capital |
| | | Maes[f] | — | 7.4 ⎪ | challenging |
| | | Alken[g] | — | 6.0 ⎭ | leaders |
| Austria | 26 | Oesterreichische Brau | — | 38.0 ⎫ 61.6 | duopoly |
| | | Steirer-Brau | — | 23.6 ⎭ | |
| Switzerland | 33 | Feldschlosschen | — | 30.1 ⎫ 49.2 | duopoly |
| | | SIBRA Group | — | 19.1 ⎭ | |
| New Zealand | 35 | Lion Breweries | — | 55.0 | quasi-monopoly |

Notes: a. A subsidiary of the South African Rembrandt/Rothmans Group.
 b. 33 per cent owned by BSN Gervais Danone.
 c. Part of San Miguel of the Philippines.
 d. 28 per cent owned by Schlitz.
 e. Includes the number 5 brewer Haacht, 38 per cent owned by Piedboeuf.
 f. Owned by Grand Metropolitan.
 g. 100 per cent owned by BSN Gervais Danone.

Source: Data computed from corporation annual reports and trade sources.

Whereas CUB and Castlemaine Tooheys held four-fifths of the beer market prior to the historic merger, CUB's marketing position *vis-à-vis* its major competitor has been enhanced. This move places considerable pressure on Castlemaine Tooheys to buy up smaller beer firms or allow itself to be annexed by a larger conglomerate, demonstrating how concentration begets further concentration the world over.

Although less pervasive than in Group A corporations, internationalisation of corporate output and trade is already on Group B's operational agenda. BSN Gervais Danone is among the top five beer producers in Spain and Belgium, and is heavily entrenched in other DME and DE markets. Its large-scale penetration of global markets is seen in its 78 per cent domination of French beer exports.[37] Other transnational forces are making their impact on the French beer market. Heineken, the Dutch beer giant, merged its French brewing interests with France's number two brewer, Brasseries et Glacières Internationales, to form a holding company commanding 25 per cent of the French market. The combined synergistic power of this transnational merger is far greater than the previously separate operations of two independent firms.

Export and production inroads into the US market have already been made by Canada's majors, a testing ground that will be used to propagate their exports into other global markets. As concentration moves apace in the remaining six countries, the largest corporations can be expected to become increasingly internationalised.

The ramifications of corporate and financial power are, however, often masked when description and analysis is circumscribed to a formal discussion of market shares. In particular, there are two types of ownership patterns that are perceived behind the bare numbers. Spain and Belgium exemplify one such pattern, where a sizeable segment of their largest corporations is owned by non-nationals. New Zealand and Australia exhibit another ownership variant through the presence of banks and financial institutions as leading shareholders. In New Zealand, the quasi-monopolistic Lion Breweries is one-fifth owned by a Singapore banker. Australia's big two provide another more complex variant. In addition to the UK's Allied-Lyons' (21 per cent) share in Castlemaine Tooheys, eight major banks and financial institutions exercise a significant control in both (Table 5.5).

Table 5.5:    Australia: Interlocking Ownership Patterns, 1980

| Corporate owners | Carlton and United Breweries[a] (per cent) | Castlemaine Tooheys (per cent) |
|---|---|---|
| Allied-Lyons (UK) | — | 14.8[b] |
| Commonwealth Trading Bank Nominees Ltd | 3.3 | 9.0 |
| Australian Mutual Provident Society | 4.2 | 5.2 |
| Mutual Life and Citizens Assurance Co. Ltd | 3.2 | 4.6 |
| National Mutual Life Assoc. of Australia Ltd | 2.9 | 1.5 |
| Colonial Mutual Life Assurance Soc. Ltd | 0.9 | 1.7 |
| City Mutual Life Assurance Soc. Ltd | 0.9 | 1.7 |
| State Superannuation Board | 1.5 | 0.9 |
| ANZ Nominees Ltd | 1.3 | 1.0 |
| Others | 81.8 | 59.6 |
| Total | 100.0 | 100.0 |

Notes:  a.  In 1981, Paribas (France) acquired 3.0 per cent.
　　　 b.  In 1981, Allied share rose to 20.9 per cent.
Source: Calculated from annual reports and information supplied by the Sydney Stock Exchange Ltd, 1981.

## Group C

There remains a final category of DMEs (Netherlands, Denmark, Ireland and South Africa) characterised by a single giant corporation which dominates a small domestic market, leading to an overspill of their beverages on the global market (Table 5.6). It is precisely the brands of three of them: Heineken, United Breweries

Table 5.6:    Concentration in the Beer Industry, 1979/80, Group C

| Country | Country rank in global beer sales | Leading corporations | Corporation rank in global beer sales | Per cent of national market |
|---|---|---|---|---|
| Netherlands | 14 | Heineken | 4 | 60.0 |
| Denmark | 20 | United Breweries | 12 | 80.0 ⎫ 90.0 |
|  |  | Faxe | — | 10.0 ⎭ |
| South Africa | 22 | South African Breweries | 17 | 97.0[a] |
| Ireland | 28 | Guinness | — | 95.0 |

Note:  a.  Refers to share of barley-based commercial beer output. Excludes substantial sorghum beer market.
Source: Data computed from corporation annual reports and trade sources.

(through its Carlsberg and Tuborg brands) and Guinness that have achieved worldwide recognition, outpacing all others.

Exported to over 140 countries, produced under licence in 17 countries and via subsidiaries and joint ventures in others, Heineken is by far the world's leading internationalised beer company.[38] Since 1955 alone, it has built 36 breweries girdling the world, 25 of them in developing countries. Almost three-quarters of its 1980 sales were outside the national market, as well as over two-thirds of its 20,500 labour force. Heineken beer is the single largest item (by volume) shipped from Europe to North America, and exceeds by over two-fifths all US imported beer sales.[39]

The company's origins go back to 1592, although it was only in 1864 that a Heineken took over the company. Today it still remains a family enterprise, with Mr Frederick Heineken owning over 50 per cent of equity capital. Like most beer companies, Heineken entered a period of sustained expansion after the Second World War, vastly speeded up after the 1968 acquisition of the Netherlands' second largest brewer, Amstel. Subsequently, Heineken came to dominate other beverage markets with the purchase of the country's largest soft drinks producer (Vrumona) and several producers and distributors of wine and distilled spirits.[40]

While no other Group C corporation has achieved Heineken's degree of internationalisation, they exhibit the same corporate contours, despite variations in their relative domination of national markets. With the merger of Carlsberg and Tuborg into United Breweries (1970), its domination of the Danish market rose to around four-fifths. Since the merger, overseas sales of this quasi-monopolist have shot up 400 per cent. With Heineken it has pioneered overseas licensing agreements in beer, and is a leader in setting up joint ventures and subsidiaries.[41]

Although formal international marketing spheres of influence may not exist, there is an almost total absence of any competitive overlap between these two international giants in the developing world.[42] United Breweries' penetration into developing country markets has been facilitated by its corporate link-up with one of the world's biggest private trading companies, the East Asiatic Company. Such marketing relationships with big trading companies is characteristic of many large alcoholic beverage corporations.

Guinness,[43] with its annexation of 96 per cent of Irish beer output, represents an even higher stage of national market domination. Ireland's commercial beer history harks back to the eighteenth century, with the setting up of the Smithwick family brewery in 1710 and that of the Guinness family in 1763. As in other countries, its beginnings were characterised by small regional brewers until the advent of the twentieth century, when Guinness's brands acquired national distribution. From that time onwards, its annexationist pace was unrelenting. By the early 1960s, it had achieved its present market dominance. Although Guinness became a public company in part to finance these massive takeovers, the Guinness family still 'controls the Group and holds about 20 per cent of the equity'.[44]

The mere 4 – 5 per cent of the national market outside Guinness's formal control is shared between two brewers: a Carling O'Keefe[45] subsidiary (Beamish & Crawford), and Murphys, with strong corporate linkages to Heineken.[46] While these two minors have made public utterances that they intend to co-operate to beat back Guinness, this must be construed as a form of corporate shadow boxing. Indeed, Guinness could force the two out of the Irish market, yet for the immediate future it seems to have decided that a semblance of competition is worth tolerating for public relations purposes, as well as to head off EEC charges of monopolistic control. Given the global power of Carling O'Keefe's parent company, it would also be unwise to eliminate a giant competitor in such a small national market. Even with these two so-called competitors, Guinness determines the pricing and marketing parameters of the Irish beer market.

Although Guinness has not yet attained the international intensity of Heineken and United Breweries, it is marketed in 140 countries, and Guinness estimates that 8 million glasses of its stout are consumed daily the world over. After having conquered the Irish market by the early 1960s, it shifted a part of its vast capital resources into an unprecedented advertising onslaught that rocketed Irish *per capita* beer consumption from 89 pints in 1960 to 216 pints in 1979. With the peaking of domestic consumption by 1975, Guinness's strategy consists primarily in redirecting its capital resources towards the annexation of larger segments of the world market. Deploying a strategy that is now fairly widespread, Guinness made significant inroads into African and Asian markets through corporate hook-ups with major world traders and brewers. In Asia, these include Hong Kong's Jardine Matheson and Sapporo, the world's fifteenth biggest brewer.

Another impetus to internationalisation has been differential overseas tax concessions and profits, glimpsed in its UK expansion (already accounting for almost half of sales). In the words of a Guinness spokesman: 'We need UK income for tax reasons.'[47] Even more compelling are the high profit rates in the former colonies of Asia and Africa. Although only 15 per cent of 1981 sales were in Africa and Asia, Guinness appropriated a staggering 36 per cent of profits from them.[48]

More than the other three Group C quasi-monopolists, Guinness has simultaneously become both vertically integrated and conglomerate. 'Every other brewer', noted a Guinness deputy chairman, 'is diversified. They are in wines, spirits, soft drinks, hotels as well as pubs. But we are confined to manufacturing, and that is the sector of brewing that is always squeezed by governments, here and abroad.' He went on to elaborate: 'We got into plastics because we were concerned about the future of Irish coopers. We are in retailing . . . because potentially it is a growth industry which should be able to buck inflation.'[49] Guinness is also one of the UK's leading manufacturers of supermarket equipment, with highly automated factories that have employed arc-welding robots since the mid-1970s.

Its beer and conglomerate activities are being meshed not only in Ireland, but in other profit centres. In Nigeria, for example, Guinness is extracting profits from its four highly remunerative breweries to proliferate its activities into a wide swathe of consumer products such as pharmaceuticals, toiletries and cosmetics in that country.

South African Breweries has followed a similar annexationist trajectory, so that by the end of the 1970s it was one of the nation's largest industrial groups with almost total control of the commercial (barley-based) beer market.[50] In their understanding of the marketing potential of the large indigenous black population, which traditionally has consumed locally brewed sorghum-based beer, South African Breweries has directed its resources at annexing a larger segment of the indigenous market. The enormous potential for corporate expansion can be glimpsed in the fact that barley-based commercial beer accounts for only 17 per cent of total South African alcohol consumption, whereas indigenous sorghum-based beer has almost a half of the market.[51] South African Breweries' attempts to penetrate into the indigenous beer market are matched by its marketing intrusions into a number of other southern African countries.[52]

## Group D

To come to grips with the salient forces at work in the developing world's beer economy, two major beer-producing countries have been selected from each of the major regions: Latin America, Africa and Asia (Table 5.7). Predictably, similar sustained levels of concentration are no less perceptible, from oligopolistic structures in Mexico and Nigeria to quasi-monopolies in Brazil, the Philippines, Kenya and Papua New Guinea.[53] Brazil's Brahma brewery is the world's fifth largest beer company.

Table 5.7:    Concentration in the Beer Industry, 1979/80, Group D

| Country | Country rank in global beer sales | in DE beer sales | Leading corporations | Corporation rank in global beer sales | Per cent of national market |
|---|---|---|---|---|---|
| Brazil | 6 | 1 | Brahma | 5 | 62 } 96 |
|  |  |  | Antarctica |  | 34 |
| Mexico | 7 | 2 | Cerveceria Modelo | 13 | 37 } |
|  |  |  | Cerveceria Cuauhtemoc | 18 | 31 } 97 |
|  |  |  | Cerveceria Moctezuma | 20 | 29 |
| Nigeria | 24 | 5 | Nigerian Breweries[a] | — | 26 |
|  |  |  | Guinness | — | n.a.[b] |
| Philippines | 27 | 6 | San Miguel | 24 | 100 |
| Kenya | 37 | 9 | Kenya Breweries | — | 71 |
| Papua New Guinea | n.a. | n.a. | Heineken | 4 | 83 } 100 |
|  |  |  | San Miguel | — | 17 |

Notes: a. 40 per cent owned by Heineken, United African Company, and other foreign interests.
  b. Not available.
Source: Data computed from corporation annual reports and trade sources.

Already, certain of the most rapidly growing DEs have embarked on import substitution policies based on foreign capital, with Nigeria a prototype of this model. In competition with Heineken, Unilever's United Africa Company, BSN Gervais Danone and Whitbread, Guinness expects to be Nigeria's biggest producer by the mid-1980s with five or six large modern breweries.

While foreign capital's role will continue to expand in the developing countries, there is an indigenous corporate force that may play, albeit peripherally, a role in the global proliferation of beer output and consumption. A handful of very powerful corporations have emerged in certain developing countries which exhibit similar conglomerate and international features as some DME-based beer giants. Conspicuous amongst these are Mexico's big three brewers and Brazil's big two. Brahma, according to the claims of its annual report, is wholly Brazilian, with plants located in twelve Brazilian states, joined to a distribution network that propels Brahma's products to over 400,000 sales outlets throughout the country. In addition to its exports, it has bottling franchises in Trinidad, Bolivia, Chile and Nigeria.[54]

A no less prominent example of the evolution of a DE-based beer TNC is San Miguel, whose creation in 1890 numbered among the first large-scale commercial breweries in South East Asia.[55] By 1914, it had already become internationalised, with exports to Guam, Hong Kong and Shanghai. Conglomeration followed with the setting up of the Royal Soft Drinks Plant (1922) and the Magnolia Ice Cream Plant (1927). Post-Second World War witnessed another expansionary outburst as the company ramified its operations into glass containers, plastics, copper mining, textiles and a wide range of food and beverage products (see Figure 5.4).

At present, San Miguel is by far the Philippines' largest food and beverage firm and the nation's fifth largest corporation. Its total monopolisation of the Philippine beer market has provided the financial resources for its expansion into Spain, Indonesia, Hong Kong and Papua New Guinea. Its ownership structure is no less highly internationalised, with over a tenth of its equity shares owned by American interests and several of its major subsidiaries partly owned by foreign capital.[56] External financial links are partnered by no less important political links on the national market. The quintessence of this meshing is the presence of the Minister of Foreign Affairs on their twelve-man board of directors.[57] The financial, marketing and political power wielded by the largest breweries, even in developing countries such as the Philippines, heralds the end of an era when relatively small corporations could break into the industry.[58]

In view of DEs' changing demographics, related to marked population growth and even faster urban growth, all developing regions (including the six selected Group D countries) clearly constitute a major potential market for beer TNCs. Their overriding strategy is not merely to raise *per capita* consumption, but to accelerate the shift away from consumption of traditional beer to their own

Figure 5.4: The San Miguel Corporation, 1981

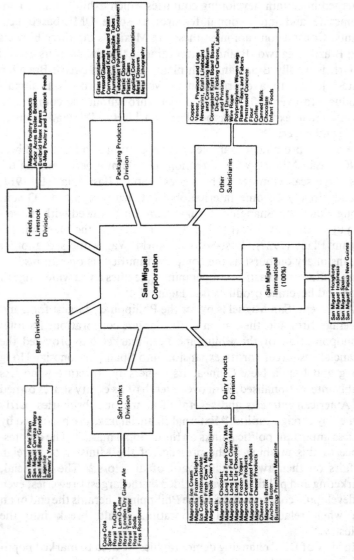

Source: San Miguel, Annual Report, 1981.

commercial brands.

Two principal groups will undoubtedly capitalise on this growing market. One is the powerful domestic entrepreneurial group within the developing countries that are heavily involved in beer and other alcoholic beverages. Another, on a scale vastly larger than the first, comprises the transnational beer companies rooted in the DMEs, whose global output and marketing capability show no signs of reaching an upper limit. As is to be expected, the public health by-product of this potentially prodigious consumption/profit upsurge augurs to be a no less marked boost in alcohol-related problems.

## Notes

1. R. J. Reynolds, *Our 100th Anniversary, 1875 – 1975* (Winston, Salem, North Carolina, 1975).

2. For the US economy alone, the price for mergers and acquisitions in 1981 surpassed $82 billion, as compared with $44 billion for all of 1980. *Wall Street Journal*, 13 January 1982.

3. Barrelage climbed from 82 million in 1950 to 176 million in 1979. See Anheuser-Busch, *Fact Book* (St Louis, 1981); and *Modern Brewery Age*, 30 March 1981. For an overview of the changes in the US beer industry, see the statement of Dr Willard F. Mueller at *Hearings on Conglomerate Mergers before the Sub-Committee on Antitrust and Monopoly of the Committee on the Judiciary*, United States Senate, Washington DC, 12 May 1978.

4. *Beverage World*, July 1981.

5. *Beverage World*, July 1981.

6. See Charles Keithahn, *The Brewing Industry*, Staff Report of the Bureau of Economics (Federal Trade Commission (FTC), December 1978); and Kenneth Elzinga, 'The Beer Industry' in Walter Adams (ed.), *The Structure of American Industry* (London, 1977).

7. This was a case of one conglomerate acquiring another conglomerate since this 53 per cent of Miller's shares was purchased from W. R. Grace, one of the largest US conglomerates, for $130 million. The remaining 47 per cent, or $87 million, was bought from the De Rance Foundation. *Modern Brewery Age*, 21 April 1980.

8. For details of R. J. Reynolds and other transnational tobacco conglomerates, see UNCTAD, *The Marketing and Distribution of Tobacco*, TD/B/C.1/205 (Geneva, 1978).

9. *Business Week*, 8 November 1976.

10. Douglas F. Greer, 'The Causes of Concentration in the US Brewing Industry', paper presented at Symposium on Advertising and the Food Systems, 6 – 7 November 1980, Virginia, USA, p. 23.

11. Loys Mather and Laurel Tucker, 'Conglomerate mergers, food advertising, and the cross-subsidization hypothesis', ibid.

12. Losses totalled $30 million between 1971 and 1976.

13. *Business Week*, 8 November 1976. Statement by Chairman of number three brewer, Schlitz.

14. Quoted in *Beer Marketer's Insights*, 1 June 1976.

15. *Miller Times*, Vol. 2, Issue 2, April – June 1976.

16. John Blair, 'The Conglomerate Merger in Economics and Law', *Georgetown*

*Law Journal*, Summer 1958.

17. John Blair, *Economic Concentration: Structure, Behavior and Public Policy* (New York, 1972), p. 51.

18. Labatt is a subsidiary of the Seagram-related conglomerate Brascan.

19. *Wall Street Journal*, 5 January 1982.

20. *Financial Times*, 4 March 1981.

21. Illustrative of this is that during the 1979/80 recession, of the 13 largest UK brewers (excluding Grand Metropolitan and the Imperial Group), 12 increased sales, 10 boosted profits and 11 increased dividends. See *Labour Research*, August 1981.

22. Whitbread alone has equity participation in eleven of them. UK Brewers Society, *Statistical Handbook* (London, 1980).

23. In 1978/9, the breakdown of alcoholic beverage sales was: pubs and hotels (57 per cent), licensed clubs (15), restaurants (3), specialised off licences (14), multiple grocers (7), independent grocers (2) and cooperatives (2). *Retail Business*, No. 271, September 1980, p. 27.

24. *Financial Times*, 4 March 1981. According to the findings of *Labour Research* (August 1981), over two-thirds of all pubs and licensed hotels are tied to large or small brewers.

25. *Wine and Spirit*, March 1980. Indicative of their involvement is that five of the big six have equity participation in the scotch whisky industry: Allied-Lyons through Teacher & Steward & Son; the Imperial Group through Saccone & Speed; Grand Metropolitan through IDV's ownership of J & B and other brands; Whitbread through Long John Distilleries; and Scottish & Newcastle through Mackinlay McPherson. *Retail Business*, June 1980.

26. Courage, at the time of its 1972 acquisition, already included eight breweries, six bottling stores, a canning plant, two maltings and three hop farms, 6,000 public houses, almost 7,000 off-licence premises, and 38 residential hotels. See Imperial Group, *The Story of the Imperial Group Limited* (London, 1977).

27. *Labour Research*, September 1981.

28. In 1980, UK beer consumption fell by 4 per cent.

29. Buckmaster and Moore, *Brewers and Distillers Newssheet*, London, May 1981.

30. This represents an upsurge in concentration since 1958, when the top four controlled 12 per cent. See Joachim Schwalbach, *Struktur und Wettbewerb in der Deutschen Brauereiindustrie*, Internationales Institut für Management und Verwaltung (West Berlin, 1982), p. 9.

31. *World Drinks Report*, 2 March 1982.

32. In calculating these percentages, ownership was defined as holding over 25 per cent of equity and being the largest shareholder. The remaining 10 per cent is owned by the state, other breweries and distilleries, and firms in other sectors. Calculated from data in Commerzbank, *Wer gehört zu wem* (Düsseldorf, 1982).

33. *Financial Times*, 5 March 1982.

34. The nation's number three brewer, Asahi, is being strengthened by a recent decision of the Finance Ministry to engineer the sale of most of Asahi's equity to the giant Asahi Chemical Corporation, and several banks and life insurance companies. In this case, the state is buttressing Asahi Brewery not for its beer capabilities, but for the application that its fermentation technology could have on the strategic bio-technology sector. *Financial Times*, 30 October 1981.

35. Although antitrust legislation was imposed on Japan by the American occupation authorities (the Anti-Monopoly Act of 1947), it did not alter permanently the highly concentrated nature of the Japanese economy. Not surprisingly, the leading antitrust administrator of the Japanese Fair Trade Commission could declare 'the history of the anti-monopoly law is a history of emasculation'. See UNCTAD, *Fibres and Textiles: Dimensions of Corporate Marketing Structure* (Geneva, 1981), p. 71.

36. *Globe and Mail* (Toronto), 24 May 1981.

37. *La Vie française*, 26 October 1981.

38. Prominent among them are 55 per cent ownership of Greece's largest brewer, and all of Italy's number two brewer. *Business Europe*, 28 November 1980; and *World Drinks Report*, 3 March 1981.

39. Extent of its penetration of the US market is gauged in its being sold in 70 per cent of all retail outlets handling alcoholic beverages. *Fortune*, 16 November 1981.

40. It also owns Duncan Gilbey and Matheson, a London distiller, and has a 20 per cent shareholding in Tomatin Distillers, a Scotch malt whisky distiller. *Financial Times*, 4 September 1982.

41. These have even overspilled the boundaries of alcoholic beverages, seen in United Breweries' 41 per cent stake in Hoechst's Indian pharmaceutical subsidiary. *Scrip*, 2 April 1977.

42. The one developing country where there appears to be some overlap is Malaysia, but it is not known whether and to what extent their activities overlap in different regions of that country.

43. Guinness's corporate headquarters are now in the UK, where it ranks after the big six as a major force on the beer market.

44. *Financial Times*, 16 December 1981.

45. Carling O'Keefe of Canada is itself a subsidiary of the Anton Rupert's South African Rembrandt/Rothmans Group conglomerate.

46. For an elaboration, see *Brewing and Distilling International*, September 1980.

47. Quoted in the *Sunday Times*, 17 January 1982.

48. Guinness, *Annual Report*, 1980.

49. Ibid. To this list could be added leisure activities, confectionery, film making and a large general trading group. See Guinness, *Annual Report*, 1981.

50. In 1980, it took over Edgars, a 450-store retail clothing chain and, along with Kirsh Industries, it controls about 20 per cent of the nation's retail market. *Financial Times*, 16 February 1982 and 25 May 1982.

51. *World Drinks Report*, 3 March 1981.

52. In 1978, National Breweries, a subsidiary of South African Breweries, was Rhodesia's biggest manufacturing company. *The Times*, 10 October 1978.

53. An idea of the complex ownership patterns involved is that Papua New Guinea's quasi-monopoly, South Pacific Brewery, is 80 per cent owned by Malayan Breweries, which in turn is 40 per cent owned by Heineken. *Asiaweek*, 9 April 1982.

54. Thailand presents but another case, where the Boon Rawd Brewery controls around nine-tenths of the domestic market, followed by another Thai brewery, Amarit, holding the remainder. *Bangkok Post*, 2 September 1982.

55. It is the world's 24th largest beer company.

56. Its Atlas Mining subsidiary, the largest mining corporation in the Philippines, is 4.6 per cent owned by Mitsubishi and 49 per cent by other foreign interests. Atlas was the nation's second most profitable company in 1980, second only to its parent firm, San Miguel. *Business Week*, 20 July 1981. Similarly, Filipro, the nation's largest coffee processor, is 51 per cent owned by Nestlé and 49 per cent by San Miguel.

57. San Miguel, *Annual Report*, 1980.

58. An attempt has been made in 1981 by a large international conglomerate to intrude into San Miguel's monopolistic preserve. Whether Mr Lucio Tan, the owner of one of the largest private commercial banks, the largest cigarette company, as well as chemical, steel and agri-business subsidiaries, can succeed is conjectural.

# 6 DYNAMICS OF WINE

It can be surmised that in the coming decade, the wine sector, still largely fragmented in most countries, will be subject to the intense pressures of economic concentration that are so pervasively a feature of the beer industry. Up to the threshold of the 1960s, global grape production and wine processing remained highly fragmented, characterised by family ownership with a long historical tradition. Within the last two decades, however, this structure has begun to crumble as large beverage corporations in several countries have moved into this sector. Concentration in wineries is highly unequal, varying from the thousands of production units in France and Italy to South Africa's quasi-monopolistic structure. Although grape cultivation has remained, as with many raw materials (i.e. cotton, cocoa, rice, etc.), highly fragmented, here again there are great variations between countries. Technologically, grape cultivation continues to be dominated by manual operations in most countries, although mechanisation is making considerable inroads.

Several major disparities in corporate market structures exist between the wine and the much more highly concentrated beer and spirits sectors. Wine is one of the rare commodities, perhaps unique, in that it is geographically branded, e.g. Champagne, Bordeaux, Porto, etc. Whereas in beer, spirits, cigarettes and many other products specific brands are promoted for individual market segments (by age, sex, income group and ethnic origin), wine producers do not have the same leverage for consumer manipulation.

Another feature of wine's geographical specificity is that it does not lend itself as easily to global marketing through licensing agreements or the setting up of subsidiaries. Although Moët-Hennessy has set up wineries in other countries, it cannot produce its native French brands there.

Consequently, exports are and will continue to remain the major medium for the globalisation of the wine industry. Herein lies one of its distinctions from beer. It is at this juncture that the importance of a new corporate agent merges, the wine importer/distributor, which in certain leading DME importing countries is an organic part of multi-billion dollar corporations.

The industry's vertical integration is at an incipient stage compared to beer, with few corporations overlapping the three basic stages of the industry: grape cultivation, wine making and distribution, including exports and imports. Linkages between the three major stages are mainly embodied in contracts between wineries and growers, and between wineries and importers. Understandably, the relative bargaining strength of these economic entities is highly unequal, with large wineries often in a monopsonistic position *vis-à-vis* a multiplicity of competitive small-scale growers with limited or no alternative sales outlets. Hence, larger wineries are strategically positioned to squeeze growers' margins.

Wine wars for larger slices of the world export market between Italy, France and the USA are already waging. As against beer, where the developing and centrally planned economies' growth potential is immense, DME wine exports face barriers in developing countries due to foreign exchange restraints and low incomes. Consequently, the economic war for markets will largely be fought out in and between the DMEs, and only peripherally for a numerically small elite in a handful of developing countries.

For analytical purposes, the major wine-producing countries have been divided into two groups designed to bring out more clearly the forces at work. It should be stressed that these analytical categories differ from those in beer.

*Group A* consists of the four major wine-producing countries in southern Europe (Italy, France, Spain and Portugal), which together have corralled three-fifths of world output. These four are characterised by relative fragmentation in ownership patterns of both grape cultivation and wineries. *Group B* consists of four rapidly growing wine-consuming countries where more advanced concentration levels, far higher than those in Group A, are evidenced at the winery stage: the USA, South Africa, the UK and Japan.

## Group A

Group A has become the centre of wine output and consumption, with the beverage playing an important cultural role in moulding life styles.[1] Wine also occupies a vital economic role, as it represents almost a tenth of total agricultural production (by value) in France and over 8 per cent in Italy.[2] While fragmentation at the grape growing and winery stages remains the norm in all four countries, there are nonetheless important variations between them.

*Italy*

By the early 1980s Italy dethroned France, the traditional wine king, emerging as the world's leading producer and exporter by volume. Its ascendancy in part stems from an extension of the cultivable area, lavish state support, and lucrative hook-ups with large wine importers, particularly in the USA. Although the foreign capital offensives to break into the Italian wine sector have momentarily been blunted,[3] embryonic forms of concentration are already observable.

Fragmentation is most evident at the first link in the wine chain, that of grape cultivation. Although an increasing number of wine growers are organising co-operatives, the average area per vineyard nevertheless is only 1 hectare (1978).

There are essentially three kinds of Italian wine: still wine, which accounts for about 95 per cent; fortified wines, 4 per cent; and sparkling wine, the remainder. Corporate concentration is by far the most advanced in sparkling wines, where the big three control about one-half of the market.[4] In the preponderant still wine sector, concentration is not so pronounced: the mass producers Folonari and Zonin each hold about 2 per cent of the market and two other large producers and one co-operative each control about 1 per cent.[5] An important vestige of the Italian wine industry that still persists today is the vast array of family-owned Italian wine companies, including the big three: Folonari, Zonin and the Marzotto subsidiary Zignago.

Italy's success on the global market has stemmed principally from two developments. Firstly, it has set up rigorous procedures and regulations on wine ingredients and quality under the general legal framework of *Denominazione di origine controllata* (DOC). As with its French counterpart, the *Appellation controlée*, this has served to ensure norms of quality and marketability. A no less significant marketing departure has been the link-ups between Italian wineries and large-scale DME corporate importers. In many cases, this involves the sale of bulk wine at very small margins to the importer who, in turn, promotes and sells at margins varying between 10 and 25 per cent on sales.[6]

These factors, wedded to relatively low labour costs, have led to Italian exports tripling their share (1970 – 80) of the US table wine market from 20 to 60 per cent. However, this sales offensive was not confined to a single segment of the wine importing market but extended across a wide range of brands. The top five US imported wine brands (1980) were of Italian origin, with the leader Riunite alone surpassing the combined aggregate US imports of French and German wines.[7]

Conquests in the global wine war are not due exclusively to 'the magic of the market place', but also to the patient and visible hand of the state, with Sicilian wine a microcosm of this evolution. Through government and EEC financial support and subsidies, there are now 110 co-operative wineries producing four-fifths of the island's wine. Such aid has facilitated the acquisition of the most advanced wine technology, thus greatly enhancing export capabilities.

Italy and France exhibit a number of common structural features. Both dominate world wine output and trade, and the industries associated with grape growing and processing in each employ hundreds of thousands, and are among the most important economic sectors in the country. Perhaps the most conspicuous difference between them has been Italy's relatively greater triumphs in annexing export markets compared to all French wine categories, with the exception of champagne.

## France

France's wine industry is among the last industries to move from relative fragmentation to increasing concentration. Although the market is large ($4 billion for *appellation controlée* wines in 1979), it is one which new entrants find difficult to penetrate without formidable financial leverage.

As in Italy, wine cultivation remains fragmented, with the bulk of vineyards owned by private family cultivators who sell to wineries through short- or long-term contracts. The wine-growing sector is indicative of the movement to greater farm consolidation in French agriculture as a whole. With mechanisation and rationalisation moving apace, the number of producers in all major farm sectors has fallen over the past decade, with the percentage drop in wine holdings second only to that in vegetables. Over the decade, the average wine holding rose from 1.8 to 2.5 hectares, indicative of a larger movement of all wine sectors in Western Europe.

The specificities of this general drive to consolidation in wine cultivation are brought out by census data (Tables 6.1 and 6.2). By 1979, 2,300 producers (half of 1 per cent of the total) owned 13 per cent of wine lands.[8]

At the winery stage, the level of concentration increases, although it is still the most fragmented beverage sector in France. Indeed, none of the top ten drinks firms in the country are wine producers,

Table 6.1:   France: Concentration Indicators of Selected Crops[a], 1970–9

|  | 1970 | 1979 | 1979 (1970 = 100) |
|---|---|---|---|
| **Fresh vegetables** | | | |
| Area[c] | 168.6 | 196.0 | 116 |
| Holdings[d] | 182.8 | 92.6 | 51 |
| Average holdings[e] | 0.9 | 2.1 | 233 |
| **Feed crops** | | | |
| Area | 4,310.0 | 4,756.0 | 110 |
| Holdings | 892.0 | 633.0 | 71 |
| Average holdings | 4.8 | 7.5 | 156 |
| **Cereals** | | | |
| Area | 9,201.0 | 9,745.0 | 106 |
| Holdings | 1,052.0 | 798.0 | 76 |
| Average holdings | 8.7 | 12.2 | 140 |
| **Vineyards** | | | |
| Area | 1,200.2 | 1,087.1 | 91 |
| Holdings | 659.9 | 429.2 | 65 |
| Average holdings | 1.8 | 2.5 | 139 |
| **Non-food crops** | | | |
| Area | 480.0 | 497.0 | 104 |
| Holdings | 125.0 | 97.0 | 78 |
| Average holdings | 3.8 | 5.1 | 134 |
| **Market gardening crops** | | | |
| Area | 45.5 | 41.3 | 91 |
| Holdings | 45.7 | 35.9 | 79 |
| Average holdings | 1.0 | 1.2 | 120 |
| **Flowers** | | | |
| Area | 6.0 | 5.9 | 98 |
| Holdings | 15.5 | 13.9 | 90 |
| Average holdings | 0.4 | 0.4 | 100 |
| **Orchards** | | | |
| Area | 261.4 | 215.1 | 82 |
| Holdings | 156.2 | 121.6 | 78 |
| Average holdings | 1.7 | 1.8 | 106 |
| **Row crops** | | | |
| Area | 1,382.0 | 1,073.0 | 78 |
| Holdings | n.a.[a] | 589.0 | n.a. |
| Average holdings | n.a. | 1.8 | n.a. |

Notes: a. Not available.

b. Ranked by growth in average holdings.

c. In 000 ha.

d. In 000 holdings.

e. In ha.

Source: Ministère de l'agriculture, *Recensement général de l'agriculture, 1979–1980* (Paris, 1981).

Table 6.2:    Vineyards: Area and Holdings, 1979

| Vineyards | less than 1 | 1 – 2 | 2 – 5 | 5 – 10 | 10 – 35 | 35 + | Total |
|---|---|---|---|---|---|---|---|
| Area[a] | 95.0 | 62.7 | 159.7 | 234.7 | 397.2 | 137.8 | 1,087.1 |
| Holdings[b] | 273.5 | 45.7 | 49.8 | 33.3 | 24.6 | 2.3 | 429.2 |
| Average holdings[c] | 0.3 | 1.4 | 3.2 | 7.1 | 16.1 | 59.9 | 2.5 |
| | | | | *in percentage* | | | |
| Area | 8.7 | 5.8 | 14.7 | 21.6 | 36.5 | 12.7 | 100.0 |
| Holdings | 63.7 | 10.7 | 11.6 | 7.8 | 5.7 | 0.5 | 100.0 |

Notes: a. In 000 ha.
b. In 000 holdings.
c. In ha.
Source: Ministère de l'agriculture (1981).

notwithstanding that wine output accounts for half of the entire beverage sector (alcoholic and non-alcoholic). There are certain wine firms, however, which are poised to acquire significantly larger market shares. By 1978, the sales of 28 firms had each surpassed the 100 million (French francs) sales mark.[9] By 1980, Moët-Hennessy and Société des Vins de France (SVF)[10] each outstripped 1 billion francs.

Spurring this drive to concentration are changing ownership patterns away from family firms towards growing ownership by big banks and other beverage firms. Some indicators of this movement include: Seagram's takeover of the number five wine firm Mumm;[11] and beverage giant Pernod Ricard's 45 per cent share of SVF. The extent of bank and finance capital's ownership of wineries is not fully known, but their influence is also substantial in their preferential loan and credit relationships.

The Bordeaux and Champagne regions may be considered a prelude to what is ahead for the overall wine sector. In rapid succession, the long-established trading houses in Bordeaux have been annexed by larger groups, both domestic and foreign. Among the leading Bordeaux houses that have fallen victim are: number two, Barton et Guestier by Seagram; number five, Calvet by Whitbread; Eschenauer and Alexis Lichine by Bass Charrington; Dourthe-Kressmann by the Dutch giant Dowe-Egbert; and De Luze by Remy Martin. The rationale of one of the acquired companies, Calvet, was that Whitbread's participation was mandatory to finance the advertising and export promotion required to market his wine in 120 countries. In this constellation of forces, only three leading

Bordeaux firms have retained an independence which is by no means guaranteed.

The confluence of these forces leading to enhanced concentration finds its highest embodiment in the champagne sector, with ten firms having over two-thirds of the market. Towering above all others is the French and global leader Moët-Hennessy, appropriating 18 per cent of the domestic market (1980) and 28 per cent of French exports.[12] This penetration is paralleled by its conglomerate extensions into cognac (with 17 per cent of the world market) and other spirits, as well as perfumes and beauty products. Symptomatic of the champagne oligopoly's power is that, despite a poor 1981 harvest, the leading firms boosted both revenues and profits, led by Moët-Hennessy with a leap in net profits of 76 per cent.

Two of Moët's recent acquisitions underline its vertical and conglomerate extensions. Vertically, it consolidated its grip on the US market by acquiring Schieffelin, one of the oldest US wine and spirits importers. Its conglomerate extensions are being buttressed by its annexation of the Christian Dior perfume and fashion business, an offshoot of the ailing textile empire of the Willot brothers.

Moët and the other leading champagne houses have consolidated their oligopolistic control over the champagne market in a major spate of mergers and acquisitions actively underpinned by the major French banks, most notably by the Banque de l'Union Européenne. This has vastly enhanced champagne's export horizons. Although champagne ranks only fifth in wine output among France's wine categories, its export volume has only been surpassed by Bordeaux wines. Export power of the champagne majors has been boosted by the intrusion of giant conglomerates such as BSN Gervais Danone, which bought out two of France's most prestigious champagne houses, Pomery and Lanson, to gain control over 5 – 6 per cent of champagne output. The importance of such takeovers is that champagne becomes a component of BSN's already gigantic international marketing in francophonic Africa and beyond.

### The Iberian Peninsula

Spain and Portugal, the two other Group A countries, present certain similarities, notably the openness of their wine sectors (as well as other economic sectors) to foreign capital. Both have created alluring foreign investment codes as compared to France and Italy. Also, both have an abundant supply of cheap and non-unionised labour that is a strong attraction to foreign capital, accentuated in

Portugal's political shift since 1976. TNCs also foresee the market-ing implications of both countries' entry into the EEC, slated for the mid-1980s.

While the Iberian peninsula's wine sectors remain more or less fragmented like those of their competitors in France and Italy, the beginnings of a foreign capital intrusion are far more blatant, seen in the transition of their four major wine-producing areas. Portugal's major wine category is port which, in both quantity and value terms, is its most important agricultural export. Of the 22 corporate groups that comprise the Port Wine Association, 7 are controlled by foreign interests, including the drinks giants Allied-Lyons, Grand Metropol-itan and Seagram.[13] Five of these are British companies, part of a trading tradition harking back to the Anglo-Portuguese Methuen treaty of 1703, which paved the way for British marketing control over Portuguese wines entering the global market. Indeed, the big five British firms currently control 60 per cent of port exports.[14]

Spain's three major wine categories: Sherry, Rioja and Penedes are witnessing the beginnings of concentration and foreign penetra-tion, albeit on a lesser scale than that of Portugal. Although sherry is still largely dominated by big family-owned firms, foreign corpora-tions have made serious attempts to take over three of the largest of these, and, in Seagram's case, they triumphed.[15] Two predominantly domestic conglomerates, Rumasa and Domecq, still produce over half the country's sherry and, in themselves, are a study of the complex imbrications between alcoholic beverages, banks and other Spanish sectors.

Over the past two decades, Señor José Maria Ruiz-Mateos has engineered an empire which has become Spain's sixth largest com-pany, as well as the country's biggest holding company. It runs a close second — in employment terms — to the nation's Compania Telefónica Nacional España.[16] Half of Rumasa's equity is owned by Señor Mateos himself, the remainder by family interests. According to certain Spanish commentators, Mateos's rapid ascent was assisted by his connections with Franco's administration through the power-ful politico-religious organisation Opus Dei; and active support from the banking system.[17] In view of Rumasa's corporate non-accountability, stemming from the absence of laws compelling private companies to disclose their balance sheet, very little is known about its financial contours.

Revealing, however, is the little that is known. Its conglomerate holdings embrace 400 firms comprising a banking network that is the nation's eighth largest.[18] Rumasa is Spain's leading operator in hotels, farming and livestock, and wine production and export. It comes in as number two in department stores, number five in construction and real estate, and number eight in the nation's insurance business. Bearing similarity to R. J. Reynolds's rationale of its conglomerate practices, Rumasa's director of overseas acquisitions emphasised:

> When the wine and spirits business became large enough, it was natural to do our own advertising instead of hiring the services of an outsider. Once we were in banking, it was logical to go into insurance . . . If, say, one of our wine companies is having a problem then the holding company will concentrate completely on that subsidiary. If it needs an infusion of capital, then the holding company will give it the money. But it will not affect the other subsidiaries . . . There is no one company in Rumasa that is large enough to affect the group as a whole.[19]

By far Spain's largest beverage group, Rumasa, owns eight of the country's top 50 beverage corporations. Merely in wine, these span fully a third of domestic sherry output; almost a third of Rioja wine, sparkling wines and Catalan table wines; four-fifths of Cordoba's Montilla; and 87 per cent of La Mancha region wines.[20] Its overseas marketing extensions include wine merchandising in the UK and Denmark, and wine warehousing in Argentina and Chile.

As a result of the government's uncovering massive skulduggery, Rumasa was nationalised in late 1982. Minister of Finance, Trade and Economics, Miguel Boyer charged Rumasa's previous management of 'a succession of irregular and unorthodox practices and of systematic concealment' of the group's operations.[21] He also noted that Rumasa's financial dealings 'are an incredible morass. There is no way of even knowing how many companies Rumasa holds.'[22] The government's investigation revealed widespread irregularities ranging from misreported assets to almost $200 million in unpaid taxes as well as dubious internal lending practices by its 18 banks.[23]

As against Rumasa's essentially family ownership, the Pedro Domecq group exhibits a more diverse, but no less powerful, ownership structure led by Banesto, Spain's biggest bank (15 per cent), Hiram Walker España (18), Pedro Domecq Mexico (12) and the Banco Internationale de Comercio (3). Domecq's extensive internationalisation is exemplified in its wholly-owned Luxembourg subsidiary, which owns 75 per cent of Pedro Domecq Mexico, the nation's largest tequilla and brandy producer.[24]

Rioja and Penedes, the other two major wine categories, have undergone some concentration, but still remain to be penetrated by foreign capital. The latter is dominated by the single family-owned firm of Torres, the single largest exporter of Spanish wines to the USA. The former has witnessed the emergence of two very large firms,[25] with sales in excess of 2 million cases annually, thus giving them a strategic vantage point on national and global markets.

Consequences of the onset of concentration and foreign penetration in Group A are already surfacing. One single corporation, Seagram,[26] whose traditional international marketing strength is not wines, operates wineries in all Group A countries and elsewhere. The implications of such corporate geographical ubiquity is that the foreign corporation is poised to respond swiftly to what it may construe as negative political developments in one country by shifting its resources to other countries. Hence the corporate internationalisation of trade and output becomes a vital element in placing a wide variety of pressures on recalcitrant political agencies and governments.

## Group B

Concentration and foreign penetration discernible in Group A have attained much higher levels in the four selected countries of Group B, ranging from a quasi-monopoly in South Africa to swiftly evolving oligopolistic market structures in the USA, the UK and Japan.[27] As against beer, where numerous primarily beer-based companies have climbed to prominence, practically all of the giant wine producers originated elsewhere, to a large extent in other beverage sectors.

While only 10 per cent of the world's wine emanates from Group B, it represents precisely those countries where wine consumption is expected to grow rapidly in the 1980s and 1990s.

### The USA

The USA is unique among the giant wine producers in its active pursuit of an import substitution policy after decades of heavy reliance on imports, particularly from Italy and France.[28] The medium- and long-term goal of American wine corporations is not only to diminish the grip of foreign imports, but equally to push up domestic *per capita* wine consumption and simultaneously encroach on the global market. The vast potential on the domestic market is seen in the meagre US *per capita* consumption of 8 litres in 1980, as against the FRG (26), Spain (65), Portugal (70), Italy (93) and France (95).

Vineyards, symptomatic of the vast strides in US land concentration, are more consolidated than those in Group A. These holdings are also highly concentrated by region, with four-fifths of grape and wine output centred in California, where wine sales topped $2 billion in 1980. Although New York State ranks a far distant second, Texas may well represent the future wine El Dorado, with tens of thousands of potential acres currently being surveyed for the day when the petroleum lands run dry.

This regional concentration is matched at the corporate level. By the end of 1979, there were 724 bonded wineries, with California alone having 450, of which 100 accounted for four-fifths of output. More to the point, however, is that wine subsidiaries of five of the largest spirits corporations had already garnered almost a half of the total wine sales by the end of the 1970s: Heublein (18 per cent), Seagram (9), National Distillers and Chemical Corporation (8), Rapid American (7), and Brown-Forman (5).[29]

Heublein broke into the market in 1969 with the acquisition of United Vintners and subsequently ploughed $100 million into upgrading and expanding their wine facilities. In addition, it also imports dozens of wine brands from Western Europe, Hungary and Japan. Seagram owns several wineries (New York and California) through its major subsidiary Paul Masson, which boosted its wine sales during the 1970s at three times the rate of the US wine market. Although purchasing the bulk of its grapes from other growers, Seagram owns 8,000 acres of grape lands. Its inventory of 45 million gallons of ageing wines is but one index of corporate power which places it in a completely different, and hence less vulnerable, category than its smaller competitors.

National Distillers and Chemical Corporation (NDCC), perhaps one of the most conglomerate of the spirits giants, was also one of the first to penetrate the wine sector with its 1967 acquisition of Almaden vineyards. Its 8 per cent control of the US wine market constitutes a trifling 10 per cent of its revenues (1980: $2.1 billion), still dominated by chemicals and metals. Through its Schenley subsidiary, Rapid American has also become paramount on wine markets, primarily through imports. Less than a third of its sales are from wine and spirits, with merchandising dominated by retailing and apparel. Finally, Brown-Forman bears comparison with Rapid American in its emphasis on wine imports. As with most of the above corporations, wine remains the company's fastest growing segment.

While penetration of the distilled spirits giants has provided the major impetus to the wine sector's expansion, two other corporations have also been central. Gallo, a family-owned company, is at once the US- and world-leading producer. Unlike the newer corporate entrants to the industry, the Gallo family enterprise (established in 1933) is a single product firm operating an integrally self-contained wine complex in California. This includes large-scale research facilities, a complete wine-making complex, a glass plant, 14 bottling lines and its own trucking firm.

Some of the reasons behind Gallo's dominance of US wine markets were neatly summed up by *Fortune*:

> Gallo enjoys operating economies at every stage of making wines. Long term contracts with hundreds of growers ensure a steady stream of grapes, produced to meticulous standards. Gallo makes its own bottles and caps, and runs its own delivery fleet. And its precision-drill sales force can march Hearty Burgundy or Chablis Blanc into discount house and general store with equal ease, gaining central displays at eye level.[30]

Coca Cola, the world's largest soft drinks manufacturer and distributor, made a vital corporate decision to enter wines in 1977. This was based on three interdependent considerations: the likelihood of wine being the fastest growing beverage segment in the 1980s; its desire to draw maximum profits from its all-embracing soft drink distribution networks in 135 countries; and the need to mitigate the batterings of price fluctuations in sugar, by far the major soft drink ingredient. Between 1977 and 1979, Coca Cola poured $111 million into wine facilities. In one year alone (1980), Wine Spectrum, its fastest growing division, recouped its investment with sales outstripping $100 million.[31] As with Philip Morris in beer, Coca Cola's entry into the wine market revolutionised merchandising, advertising and promotion, and the upshot was no less predictable: swift liquidation of smaller wineries.

Six years after its dramatic entry into the wine market, Coca Cola sold its wine holdings to another alcohol giant, Seagram. This pushed Seagram from number four to number two in US wine behind Gallo.

By the very nature, mechanisms and trajectory of transnational capitalism, it would have been unrealistic to expect that US corporate dominance of its own domestic wine market would remain long unchallenged. Whereas wine has entered the USA for centuries, a wholly new development in recent years has been the arrival of foreign capital. Baron Philippe de Rothschild (owner of Château Mouton-Rothschild), Moët-Hennessy and Piper-Heidsieck, three of the leading French and world wineries, have stormed the US market through joint ventures in wineries and takeovers of grape lands. By the end of 1983, Moët-Hennessy's American operations topped $200 million yearly, about a third of its total sales.

Differential stages in corporate capital's evolution are discernible in a comparison of the oligopolistic US market and that of South Africa where, as in beer, a quasi-monopoly has been forged.

## The Republic of South Africa

In 1979, three quasi-independent corporate forces existed in the South African wine sector. Dominating the grape cultivation stage was the Kooperative Wijnbouwers Vereniging (KWV) with its 6,000 independent grape growers. It has become one of the Republic's most powerful pressure groups or, in the words of a South African member of parliament: 'the wine lobby is more powerful than the oil lobby in Washington'.[32] One of the mainsprings of KWV's power springs from its monopoly on wine exports, as well as its regulation of production and prices.

South African Breweries (SAB), the beer quasi-monopolist, was the second of the big three, with its dominant control over three-quarters of South African wine production. There was yet another giant whose global tentacles embraced $8.5 billion (1980) in tobacco, liquor and other sales: Anton Rupert's Rembrandt Group.[33] This highly secretive group is owned by a series of four complex interlocking holding companies. Its Rothman's Tobacco Holdings has overseas cigarette subsidiaries in a wide range of countries. Its operations include no less complex corporate link-ups with Philip Morris, one of the world's leading alcohol and tobacco corporations.

Figure 6.1 gives a rough indication of Rembrandt's global operations, including two major international alcohol subsidiaries: Carling O'Keefe breweries (headquartered in Toronto, Canada)

Figure 6.1: The Rembrandt/Rothmans Group, *c.* 1980

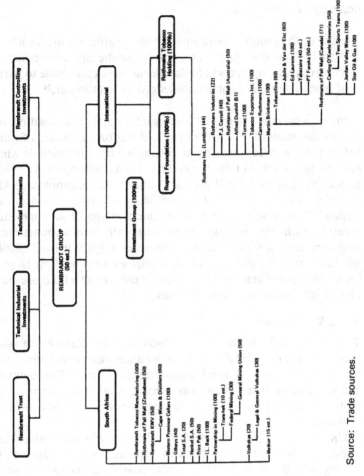

Source: Trade sources.

and Jordan Valley Wines. A gauge of its non-accountability, as noted by *Fortune*, is that

> many of the group's operations are low profile ventures, such as those in Zimbabwe and Zaire. Some, like the cigarette company Rupert says he operates in Malaysia and the export trade to parts of Black Africa, are not acknowledged by Rembrandt.[34]

In an economy where the concentration and centralisation of capital has attained a very high pitch, it was only a matter of time before the big three were driven to combine their formidable wine arsenals into what, in fact, has become a quasi-monopoly. In 1980, fusion gave birth to Cape Wine and Distillers, with Rembrandt, SAB and KWV each owning a 30 per cent share of equity.[35] Hence, the Republic's wine sector has now become a model of monopolistic control, with the techniques of corporate non-accountability enshrined in its complex holding companies. Cape Wine and Distillers has further extended its alcohol empire and is now the largest importer of proprietary brands of scotch and accounts for more than half of all whisky sold in the Republic.

## The UK and Japan

These two island nations at the extremities of the Euro-Asian land mass, while still insignificant wine producers and consumers, are among the fastest growing wine-consuming countries. The common denominator of their wine sectors is that they are being restructured by the intrusion of large alcoholic beverage corporations rooted in beer and spirits.

UK wine distribution, which is almost exclusively based on imports, is two-fifths controlled by eight companies. Paramount among the eight are four of the big six brewers,[36] as well as two giant supermarket chains: Sainsburys and Marks & Spencer. Likewise in Japan, three of the big six grape wine producers[37] are from other alcohol sectors: Sapporo Breweries, the smaller Toyo brewing company and Suntory. This giant's wine history goes back to 1907 and, according to its own claims, 'our total product line has been expanded as have our production capabilities and vineyards, which are the largest in the Orient'.[38]

Analytically relevant in the history of concentration is that, in all countries, its movement in one sector often inflects the movement in another. This is certainly the case when products are substitutable.

To the extent that concentration in beer and distilled spirits moves apace, corporate annexationist pressures will also build up in the wine sector.[39]

## Notes

1. In 1980, 46 per cent of the world's wine was consumed in these four countries. Calculated from figures of Office International de la Vigne et du Vin, in *World Drinks Report*, 13 October 1981.

2. Source EEC, *La Situation de l'agriculture dans la communauté, rapport 1979* (Brussels, 1980). There are significant variations in the relative importance of table and quality wine, with the former being far more important in Italy, whereas in France (as in the FRG and Luxembourg), quality wines occupy a much larger role.

3. Most notably, Grand Metropolitan's subsidiary IDV and Seagram.

4. Cinzano, Gancia and Riccadonna, see *Marketing in Europe*, October 1979.

5. Still wine production can be broken down as follows: 42 per cent produced by independent wine growers or communal wine cellars, 38 per cent by co-operatives and 20 per cent by industrial enterprises. In 1978, there were 708 wine cellars and 132 industrial wine producers. *Marketing in Europe*, October 1979, p. 76.

6. The Chairman of the Villa Banfi wine company, the source of these margin figures, would not disclose specific profit figures. See *Fortune*, 30 November 1981.

7. Italian wineries have by no means restricted their marketing efforts to the USA. Indicative is the 1981 deal between McGuinness Distillers of Canada, a subsidiary of Nabisco Brands (a major US food processor), and Corovin, a marketing agency for a group of 23 Italian co-operative wineries. Although this is the first major contract between Italian wineries and a Canadian importer, it is suggestive of the corporate forces that have now been set in motion.

8. Despite its minimal connections to the global market, Swiss vineyards have been subject to the same forces of concentration. Over a seven-decade span (1905 – 75), the average vineyard area rose by 59 per cent, notwithstanding a drop in total area under cultivation from 25,000 to 12,000 hectares. Calculated from data in *Crédit Suisse Bulletin*, Autumn 1980.

9. See study by Charles Arnaud and Alain Berger, 'Le Négoce du Vin français: Son evolution and son avenir', quoted in *Revue vinicole internationale*, June-July 1980.

10. In 1980, SVF alone controlled 14 per cent of total table wine sales and 4 per cent of the national wine market.

11. Mumm's chairman, Alain de Gunzburg, now sits on Seagram's board of directors.

12. See Moët-Hennessy, *Annual Report*, 1980. It is a family enterprise with two thirds of its equity capital controlled by four families: Moët, Chandon, Hennessy and Mercier. See *Agra Alimentation*, 28 August 1980.

13. Allied-Lyons controls Cockburns and Martinez Gassiot; Grand Metropolitan, through its subsidiaries IDV and Harveys, controls Croft, Delaforce and Morgan; while Seagram controls Robertson and Sandeman. Two other groups are controlled either by French or by joint Franco-British interests. Attempts to take over other major Portuguese wine companies have thus far been unsuccessful. The major one involved Whitbread's attempted takeover of the Guedes family stake of the Sogrape Group, owner of Portugal's most international wine brand, Mateus.

14. TNCs also already control 3 per cent of Portugal's commercial vineyards, and the Portuguese Wine Exporters Association predicts that, within a short time span,

around 10 per cent of port exports will originate from TNC holdings. *Le Monde*, 15 December 1981.

15. A notable failure was Philip Morris's and Pernod Ricard's attempt to take-over the *bodega* (winery) Terry, which managed to escape the grip of foreign acquisition by selling out to a Catalan financial group.

16. *Vision*, January 1981.

17. *Financial Times*, 20 January 1978.

18. These include: banking (21); stock exchange brokers (12); insurance (3); financing (16); food (4); cattle raising (13); beverages (29); shipbuilding (4); construction (9); building societies, property promoters and developers (78); tourism (5); advertising and other services (6); commercial activities (32); and the arts (7), etc. *Vision*, January 1981.

19. *Management Today*, September 1980.

20. *World Drinks Report*, 21 December 1981; and *Financial Times*, 3 June 1980.

21. *Financial Times*, 2 March 1983.

22. *Business Week*, 14 March 1983.

23. Señor Boyer also charged that 'Rumasa's banks were lending an average of 62 per cent of their risk capital to member companies. In many cases, dummy loan corporations were set up.' (Ibid.)

24. It also has operations in Italy, Colombia, the Netherlands, Panama and Venezuela. *Financial Times*, 27 March 1982.

25. It is one of the ironies of history that these two large Rioja firms (Berberana and Paternina) are competing successfully with French wines, since it was the transfer of French grapes and wine-making techniques that launched wine growing there a century ago.

26. Its corporate profile is examined in the subsequent section on distilled spirits.

27. Australia's wine sector has also moved in the direction of oligopoly. As early as 1972, the Australian *Financial Review* noted:

> South Australia's traditional family wine industry is no more. For during the past two years no fewer than 13 of them have been swallowed up by larger companies. And in two cases there have been double takeovers. With the takeovers have come a considerable inflow of foreign capital, business ruthlessness and marketing expertise.

Quoted in Len Fox, *Multinationals Take Over Australia* (Sydney, 1981), p. 160. Since then, two institutional forces have furthered their penetration into Australian wine: large Australian brewers and TNCs, including: Rothmans, Philip Morris, Grand Metropolitan through its subsidiary Gilbeys Australia Ltd., Reckitt & Coleman, Heinz Foods, Dalgety-Spillers, Rank Hovis McDougall, the Inchape Group and Amatil.

28. The origins of US wine making hark back to the sixteenth century when indigenous grapes were fermented by early settlers. Modern wine making, however, dates back to 1861 when a Hungarian immigrant transported cuttings from Europe to California.

29. For an amplification, see annual reports and 10-K forms of these companies.

30. *Fortune*, 18 April 1983.

31. Of the ten biggest wine producers, Coca Cola's Wine Spectrum recorded the largest 1981 growth (24 per cent) in sales by volume. *International Herald Tribune*, 15 April 1982.

32. *Eurofood*, 10 August 1978.

33. As of 1979, Rembrandt and its affiliates exercised varying degrees of control over 449 retail outlets.

34. *Fortune*, 10 August 1981.

35. A key element in this reorganisation involved Rembrandt selling its brewing subsidiary to SAB. This re-established the latter's beer monopoly in exchange for

Rembrandt getting management control of Cape Wine and Distillers. See *Brewing and Distilling International*, January 1980.

36. Descriptive of this power complex is that Bass alone imported and marketed 40 – 50 per cent of Italian wine sold in the UK. *Financial Times*, 15 December 1977.

37. Japan's other wine sector, the centuries-old rice-based sake industry, is also becoming more concentrated, but for different reasons. The country's 2,600 sake producers (1980 sales: $5.7 billion), whose numbers exceed those of any other single industrial sector in Japan, have been losing market shares to the far more concentrated beer and spirits sectors. As smaller sake producers are liquidated, a few medium-sized companies have emerged, led by Okura Shuzo (1980 sales: $300 million), with around 8 per cent of the total market. See *Business Japan*, August 1982, p. 57.

38. Suntory Limited, *The World of Suntory* (Osaka, 1980), p. 12.

39. Likewise, historically, concentration in a given sector in one country has at times engendered concentration in that same sector in other countries. The 1925 merger of the German chemical giants BASF, Bayer and Hoechst into IG Farben swiftly triggered mergers within the British chemical industry, which created Imperial Chemical Industries (ICI) in 1926. See UNCTAD, *Fibres and Textiles*, p. 141.

# 7 DYNAMICS OF DISTILLED SPIRITS

From a corporate perspective, distilled spirits bear far greater similarity to the beer than to the wine sector. Comprising several major categories, distilled spirits are highly heterogeneous due to their widely divergent raw material inputs. In most distilled spirits categories, relatively high concentration levels are perceived in leading DMEs,[1] and this has speeded up since the onset of the latest global economic crisis in the late 1970s.[2] With few exceptions, the largest firms produce a wide product range, exhibited in Seagram's output of whisky, rum, gin, vodka and liqueur.

As in beer, many of the giants are vertically integrated from raw material processing through distillation, brand ownership and marketing. With the possible exception of certain UK Scotch whisky producers, most have already conglomerated, with petroleum and natural gas holdings figuring prominently in the total assets of several.

Further, all the major distilled spirits firms are internationalised, and many are contractually linked with the giant multi-commodity traders as their importers/distributors.[3] For certain of the latter, trade in alcohol was a logical extension of trading in other primary commodities. E. D. & F. Man, one of the world's biggest sugar traders, is also one of the major rum shippers. Others, such as the Japanese Sogo Shosha (general trading companies), span virtually the entire gamut of commodities output, with Mitsubishi alone merchandising 25,000 commodities.

For analytical and expository purposes, the categories used in the preceding beer and wine sectors are inappropriate for distilled spirits. Rather, the distilled spirits industry can best be designated as comprising three geo-corporate complexes girdling North America, Western Europe and Japan. Characteristically, the paramount corporations that constitute each geo-corporate complex have penetrated most countries that are contiguous to their corporate headquarters. This, of course, by no means suggests that a distilled spirits corporation's marketing reach is confined exclusively to its own geo-corporate complex, since their operations are internationalised. Yet, in almost all cases, the bulk of their sales and profits derive from their specific geo-corporate complex.

## North America: The Geo-corporate Complex

Five corporations, with combined 1980 sales outstripping $10 billion, dominate the North American geo-corporate complex, with two headquartered in Canada and three in the USA.[4] Headquarter location as an indicator of the locus of ultimate decision-making power, however, can be misleading. Despite its Canadian head-quarters (Montreal), Seagram's US sales were over eight times larger than its Canadian sales. Its chairman of the board has been a US citizen since 1955. Beyond North America, the big five's penetrative power is pervasive in Latin America where they rank amongst the majors in wine and distilled spirits.

### Table 7.1:   US Distilled Spirits: Corporate Profile, 1980

| Company | Per cent of total market | Leading brands (category) | Brand ranking[b] |
|---|---|---|---|
| Seagram | about 20 | Seagram's 7 Crown (blend) | 3 |
| (also | | Seagram's VO (Canadian) | 4 |
| Paul Masson wine | | Seagram's Gin (gin) | 9 |
| Christian Bros wine) | | Kessler (blend) | 21 |
| | | Christian Bros. Brandy (brandy) | 22 |
| | | Calvert Extra (blend) | 28 |
| | | Chivas Regal (scotch) | 35 |
| NDCC | n.a. | Windsor Supreme (Canadian) | 13 |
| (also | | Gilbey's Gin (gin) | 16 |
| Almaden wine) | | Kamchatka (vodka) | 19 |
| | | Gilbey's Vodka (vodka) | 23 |
| | | Old Grand Dad (bourbon) | 31 |
| | | Old Crow (bourbon) | 34 |
| Heublein | about 10 | Smirnoff (vodka) | 2 |
| | | Popov (vodka) | 7 |
| | | Black Velvet (Canadian) | 18 |
| | | Arrow Cordials (cordial) | 33 |
| | | Club Cocktails (cocktails) | 36 |
| Brown-Forman | n.a. | Jack Daniels (bourbon) | 8 |
| | | Canadian Mist (Canadian) | 11 |
| | | Early Times (bourbon) | 20 |
| | | Southern Comfort (cordial) | 30 |
| Hiram Walker | n.a. | Canadian Club (Canadian) | 5 |
| | | Kahlua (liqueur) | 25 |
| | | Ten High (bourbon) | 27 |
| | | Hiram Walker Cordials (cordial) | 32 |
| Others | n.a. | | |

Note: a. Not available.
    b. Ranked by volume sold in USA.
Source: Computed from data in *Impact*, 15 February 1981.

Already, these big five extend control over half of the US market.[5] Three have seized three-quarters of the market in the province of Ontario, suggestive of their wider control of the Canadian market.[6] McGuiness, a subsidiary of a US agri-business giant (Nabisco Brands), with around 11 per cent of the Canadian market, is yet another significant economic agent.[7] Their dominance in several spirits categories is depicted in their overwhelming presence among top US brands (Table 7.1).

On the surface it might appear that the big five suffered setbacks over the past decade as the relative share of distilled spirits in total North American alcoholic beverage consumption slumped. In reality, however, the big five from the late 1960s on tended to offset distilled spirits' relative decline by moving into the wine sector. When wine consumption subsequently outpaced that of spirits for the first time in US history (1980), they stood in the front ranks of the gainers (Table 7.2).

Table 7.2:    USA: Distilled Spirits versus Wine, 1970 – 80

| Category | Share of market (per cent) | |
|---|---|---|
| | 1970 | 1980 |
| Bourbon | 22.9 | 13.9 |
| Scotch | 13.0 | 12.9 |
| Canadian | 9.0 | 12.5 |
| Blends | 19.9 | 8.9 |
| Other | 0.3 | 0.3 |
| *Total whisky* | *65.1* | *48.5* |
| Vodka | 12.4 | 19.0 |
| Gin | 9.9 | 9.5 |
| Cordials | 4.9 | 7.8 |
| Rum | 2.9 | 7.1 |
| Brandy | 3.5 | 4.1 |
| Other | 1.3 | 4.0 |
| *Total non-whisky* | *34.9* | *51.5* |
| Total consumption of spirits (millions of gal.) | 369.9 | 452.0 |
| Total consumption of wines (millions of gal.) | 267.4 | 476.0 |

Source:  Compiled from data of Clark Gavin Associates Inc., and the Wine Institute.

*Seagram: A Case Study*

Seagram embodies concentrated corporate power. It straddles a vast array of alcoholic beverages, with about 150 distilled spirits brands and 300 brands of wines, champagne, port and sherry sold in over 175 countries and territories.[8] Via the Bronfman family's complex holding company operations, Seagram is also linked to a major producer of beer and an imposing spectrum of other commodities.

*Foundations.* 'The concentration of wealth [noted the *Financial Times*] in the hands of a relatively small number of families and individuals makes Canada almost unique in the industrialized world . . . The power of this elite is formidable. Since 1978, a spate of bids, deals and takeovers has underlined the enormous resources they have at their disposal. Now they are turning their attention to the US and beyond.'[9]

The Bronfman dynasty is at the apex of this power structure.[10] Its roots go back to 1889 with the arrival in Canada of Ekiel Bronfman, the founder of the dynasty. His Manitoba hotel became the launching pad for the small-scale sale of alcoholic beverages. The prosperity years of the First World War (1914 – 18) witnessed the extension of the family business through a novel merchandising technique: liquor sales via the postal services by two of Ekiel's sons, Samuel and Allan.

By 1928, operations were further extended by the takeover of distiller Joseph E. Seagram & Sons which, during the prohibition years, vastly extended its capital base as a vital supplier to US bootleggers.[11] In the ensuing decades, abetted by massive acquisitions and its own expansion programme, Seagram was to be metamorphosed into the world's largest distilled spirits corporation and a major wine producer with 26 wine operations around the world.

*Overseas Extensions.* Seagram has backward and forward linkages underpinning both its spirits and wine activities. As a feeder base to its distilleries, it has become one of the largest operators of grain-storage facilities in North America.[12] From its North American vantage point, Seagram was to ramify its operations into every continent:

1. In Latin America, Seagram is one of the biggest whisky producers in Brazil through its locally produced brand Natu Nobilis;[13] and in Argentina it has acquired a 15 per cent share in the country's leading producer of fine wines.
2. In Western Europe, expansion is occurring through the buy-out

of some of the oldest family-owned firms, as well as the implantation of subsidiaries: in port and sherries, through the annexation of Sandeman;[14] in whisky, through the buy-out of the Glenlivet Distilleries; in the FRG, where three of its spirits brands rank among the top 100; and in practically all southern European countries through its established wineries.

3. It established an Asian beachhead through its Robert Brown joint venture with Japan's Kirin brewery.[15] Elsewhere in Asia it has joined its resources with those of major domestic entrepreneurs which facilitated the conquest of ever larger segments of their rapidly growing markets.

4. In the Australian region, the impact of their power will now be felt by the takeover of New Zealand's one and only whisky producer.

*Conglomerate Ramifications.* The rationale of Seagram's acquisitions was voiced by its Chairman, Edgar Bronfman, as 'building on what my father accomplished'.[16] Such filial loyalty, however, does not explain the specific and changing forms that these have assumed over the years. Conglomerate annexationism has been planned and executed through secretive and legally complex holding companies not basically dissimilar from the design of Anton Rupert's Rembrandt/Rothmans group in South Africa.

At the epicentre of the Bronfman empire are two gargantuan holding companies: CEMP Investments and Edper Investments.[17] The former controls Seagram; Cadillac-Fairview, one of North America's largest real estate developers; extensive oil, natural gas, coal and uranium resources; and a huge portfolio of shares in other TNCs. Edper is more complex in that many of its subsidiaries fall under the umbrella of its own holding company, Brascan, with ownership extending over a wide swathe of natural resources, service and consumer product corporations, including the John Labatt brewing company. While CEMP and Edper are legally distinct entities, they are imbricated in a multitude of ways through interlocking directorates and extended family ties.

*The Escalating Stakes.* Seagram surged into the 1980s with unprecedented acquisition resources of over $4 billion, in large part due to its massive cash flows and a $2.3 billion windfall from sale of its oil and gas interests to Sun company.[18] Its launching of several takeover wars has been made possible by its formidable investment banking connections in Goldman, Sachs and Company; Lazard Freres; and a large number of other financial institutions. Pinpointing the quintessence of its linkages to finance capital, the 1981 annual report noted that

> by December, Seagram's financial staff had arranged the acquisition financing — a limited recourse $1.62 bn. facility — and an unsecured $1.38 bn. revolving credit agreement. Thirty-one banks participated, an unusually small number for such a large credit, and the time in which the financing was accomplished was unusually short.

Summarising the annexationist blueprint, its chairman announced that its goals were all-embracing 'except for atomic energy and the steel business'.[19] The offensive began with the $2.13 billion bid for St. Joe Minerals that was countered by the latter's claim that Seagram's offer was 'false and misleading in its failure to disclose required information about the integrity of the Seagram's management and about the Bronfman family members and associates which control Seagram'. It also contended that Seagram's bid failed to mention 'a long history' of illegal payments and political contributions, Federal tax and liquor violations 'including 33,000 offenses in Pennsylvania alone'.[20]

Although its onslaught was blunted by the abortive attempt to acquire St. Joe's, Seagram immediately redeployed its forces to seize Conoco, the number nine US petroleum company and parent of the Consolidated Coal Company. While formally losing what was the biggest corporate annexation in history ($7.6 billion) to Du Pont de Nemours, it nonetheless led to Seagram carving out a 21 per cent stake in Du Pont,[21] a larger voting bloc than the hundreds of Du Pont heirs combined. Henceforth, the fate and fortunes of big alcohol were to be fused with big chemistry. Jubilantly, Seagram's 1981 annual report contended that 'the combined Du Pont and Conoco now ranks as North America's seventh largest industrial corporation, a company with combined revenues of $32 billion and assets of $22 billion'. To which could be added that the Du Pont – Seagram corporate complexes are now closely intermeshed, with each firm having their respective chairman on the other's board of directors.

Because Seagram represents a more mature form of vertical and conglomerate extension so characteristic of the top five distilled spirits corporations, the subsequent section will not cover extensively their individual case histories. Rather, exposition will be focused so as to bring out the structural variations among the lesser corporate constellations in this alcohol segment.

## The Lesser Majors

Whereas three of the lesser majors trail Seagram in aggregate sales by a relatively small margin, their orbits are significantly smaller than Seagram because of the latter's powerful holding companies and its coupling with Du Pont. Thus, the lesser majors follow the dictates of a global market largely shaped by Seagram. It now appears striking that internationalisation and conglomeration have become a prerequisite for growth and survival.

With the exception of Brown-Forman, the lesser majors are heavily conglomerated. In their own right, NDCC and Hiram Walker[22] could be designated as major petroleum companies and the latter has now become entrenched in wineries in California and France, as well as wine importing. Hiram Walker shares with Seagram an ownership structure ruled by one of Canada's wealthiest families. Apart from Hiram Walker Resources, the Reichmann family's major corporate holding is the conglomerate Olympia and York Developments. With assets of around $12 billion, it is one of North America's largest real estate companies.[23]

Overnight R. J. Reynolds's $1.4 billion takeover of Heublein (1982) propelled it into one of the world's most powerful alcoholic beverage TNCs (Figure 7.1). Even prior to its buy-out, Heublein owned the largest US vodka brand, and the second largest wine operation. Since the acquisition, Heublein has been joined to one of the world's biggest agri-business concerns, Del Monte, to form a new beverage and food division. Reynolds was attracted to Heublein's major presence in brand name consumer goods, especially outside the USA, crystallised in Heublein's contention that 'overseas, where our business, in recent years, has been growing two to three times the rate of that in the US, we see opportunities abounding'.[24] With due allowance for sectoral variations, this contention portrays a process that increasingly holds for both unprocessed and industrial commodities, particularly those consumer product lines where domestic markets are approaching saturation. Thus, internationalisation has its own compulsive logic which inescapably embraces both major and minor corporations.

Overseas operations already provide Heublein with 22 per cent of

Figure 7.1: R. J. Reynolds Plus Heublein, 1981

The merger would create a $13.8 billion company based on 1981 sales; segment percentage data are shares of this combined company's sales

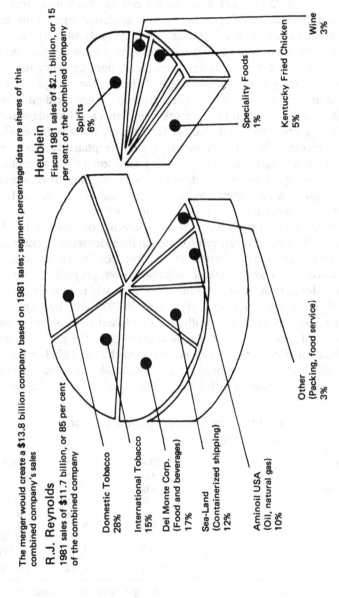

## R.J. Reynolds
1981 sales of $11.7 billion, or 85 per cent of the combined company

Domestic Tobacco 28%

International Tobacco 15%

Del Monte Corp. (Food and beverages) 17%

Sea-Land (Containerized shipping) 12%

Aminoil USA (Oil, natural gas) 10%

Other (Packing, food service) 3%

## Heublein
Fiscal 1981 sales of $2.1 billion, or 15 per cent of the combined company

Spirits 6%

Wine 3%

Speciality Foods 1%

Kentucky Fried Chicken 5%

Source: *New York Times*, 30 July 1982.

revenues and 25 per cent of operating profits. Such indicators of internationalisation hold true not only for its alcohol operations, but no less so for its other product lines. The fact that Heublein produces a vast spectrum of wines and spirits means that it is ideally positioned to meet demand for the fastest-growing alcohol category in each national market at a specific moment. In Brazil, for example, where vodka and certain wines have been growing at double digit rates, Heublein has locked into those market segments and has adapted its marketing goals to specific social formations, notably those with higher income. One of its rationales is that 'emphasis is also being placed on strengthening [our] leading position in the premium-priced whisky category, which is relatively immune to economic slowdown',[25] a marketing strategy no less relentlessly pursued by other distilled spirit TNCs in developing countries.

The scale and profitability of such internationalisation by the biggest TNCs become self-reinforcing on their domestic operations, giving them an edge over smaller competitors confined to the domestic market. Such corporate internationalisation, propelled by multi-million dollar promotion, becomes even more self-reinforcing in the age of mass communication and tourism. In 1979, over half a billion tourists spent more than $80 billion, a significant share of which was on alcohol. Data on international tourism over the past 15 years provides an indicator of its exponential growth (Tables 7.3 and 7.4). Invariably, in the major airports, airlines, hotels, bars and casinos, tourists are confronted with familiar brands of the alcohol majors.

Table 7.3:    International Tourist Arrivals at Frontiers, 1964 – 79[a] ('000 persons)

| Region | 1964 | 1975 | 1979 |
|---|---|---|---|
| Europe | 77,000 | 221,567 | 386,926 |
| Latin America | 4,000 | 78,766 | 82,788 |
| North America | 19,000 | 74,763 | 76,912 |
| East Asia & Pacific | 2,000 | 11,034 | 16,888 |
| Africa | 1,600 | 5,114 | 6,135 |
| Middle East | 2,100 | 3,961 | 5,497 |
| South Asia | ★[b] | 1,649 | 1,969 |
| Total | 105,700 | 396,854 | 577,115 |

Notes: a. Includes excursionist and cruise passenger arrivals for 1975 and 1979.
    b. Included in figure for East Asia and Pacific.

Source: International Union of Official Travel Organizations, *World Travel* (June 1965), p. 8; World Tourism Organization, *Regional Breakdown of World Tourism Statistics, 1975 – 1979* (Madrid, 1981).

**Table 7.4:    International Tourism Receipts[a] 1964 – 79 ($ million)**

| Region | 1964 | 1975 | 1979 |
|---|---|---|---|
| Europe | 6,000 | 26,363 | 53,974 |
| North America | 1,700 | 6,410 | 10,345 |
| Latin America | 1,500 | 3,809 | 7,141 |
| East Asia & Pacific | 600 | 2,524 | 5,683 |
| Africa | 250 | 1,127 | 1,692 |
| Middle East | 180 | 438 | 1,283 |
| South Asia | ★[b] | 329 | 710 |
| Total | 10,230 | 41,000 | 80,828 |

Notes: a. Excluding international fare receipts.
   b. Included in figure for East Asia and Pacific.
Source: International Union of Official Travel Organizations, *World Travel* (June 1965), p. 8; World Tourism Organization, *Regional Breakdown of World Tourism Statistics, 1975 – 1979* (Madrid, 1981).

## Western Europe: The Geo-corporate Complex

Although much of Western Europe is formally unified through the EEC, its distilled spirits market has not yet attained the level of corporate cohesion as evidenced in North America. Whereas the North American big five have plants spread across frontiers, the Western European majors have interpenetrated each others' markets almost exclusively via exports. This, in part, is imputable to fairly distinctive national consumption patterns in Western Europe, with whisky dominant in the UK, brandy and aniseed-based drinks the leaders in France, and brandy on top in the FRG. Such distinctive consumption patterns, however, in themselves are in no way immutable as they are continuously subject to an unrelenting barrage of transnational advertising.

Analysis is centred on the major distilled spirit producing countries: the UK, France and the FRG.

### The UK

For centuries, the UK has been the centre of the world's largest distilled spirits category: whisky. Notwithstanding that the UK's industrial export shares have been sharply eroded in almost all product lines, whisky exports have grown markedly in the post-war period, so that by 1980 their value was almost £900 million, or 2 per cent of export revenues.

Major institutional shifts have been a catalytic factor in the industry since the Second World War. Basically, these consist of three major external economic groupings that penetrated the UK scotch whisky industry: TNCs, brewers and conglomerates (Table 7.5). Led by Seagram and Hiram Walker (each with nine distilleries by 1979), TNCs had seized one-fifth of UK output, an overriding factor in the 1980 decision of the Monopolies and Mergers Commission in rejecting[26] Hiram Walker's takeover bid of Highland Distilleries. This pinpoints that no 'independent' Scotch whisky company remains invulnerable to the annexationist drives of these three corporate phalanxes. A study of the UK domestic whisky market suggests that TNCs have not used their whisky implantations in Scotland thus far to penetrate significantly the UK market. The ten largest UK brands are still owned by UK companies, with Distillers Company Ltd (DCL)[27] and Arthur Bell with half of the market. Rather, takeovers of prominent Scottish distilleries offer TNCs the locational advantages of duty-free entry into EEC countries, as well as control over enormous ageing inventories of distinguished brand names.

Table 7.5:    Control of UK Distilleries, 1979

| | Number of malt distilleries | Number of grain distilleries |
|---|---|---|
| Leading UK 'independent' distillers | 78 | 12 |
| DCL | 45 | 5 |
| Highland | 5 | – |
| Invergordon | 5 | – |
| Arthur Bell | 4 | – |
| William Grant | 3 | 1 |
| Others | 16 | 6 |
| TNCs | 24 | 1 |
| Seagram | 9 | – |
| Hiram Walker | 8 | 1 |
| Others | 7 | – |
| UK Brewers | 8 | 1 |
| Whitbread | 4 | 1 |
| Others | 4 | – |
| Conglomerates | 7 | 0 |
| Grand Metropolitan | 4 | – |
| Lonrho | 3 | – |
| Total | 117 | 14 |

Source: Compiled from: UK Monopolies and Mergers Commission, *Hiram Walker-Gooderham & Worts Limited and the Highland Distilleries Company Limited: A Report on the Proposed Merger* (London, HMSO, 1980).

Indeed, the dimensions of the global market dwarf the UK's, as over four-fifths of all Scotch whisky is exported. Whereas earlier, Scotch whisky was the paramount force on global whisky markets, by the mid-1970s its share had slumped to one-third after marketing onslaughts of American whisky (26 per cent); Canadian (15); Japanese (14); and Indian (5). While formally correct, this geo-market segmentation breakdown masks the imbrications of corporate power that straddle these categories since, for example, a fifth of so-called 'Scotch' whisky is not produced by UK-based corporations.

Significant also is the changing morphology of the UK market in the global whisky economy. Not only is its ownership structure changing, but what is striking in a country that pioneered the industrial revolution is the perceptible shift from manufactured whisky exports to exports of a primary feed stock: bulk malt whisky. The rationale behind this shift is that the UK faces whisky-importing countries that are protecting or developing their own distilling and bottling industries. Thus, import substitution is carried out by establishing high tariff and non-tariff barriers on bottled whisky, while admixing[28] bulk malt imports with locally distilled spirits.[29] Japan and Spain are the two leading practitioners, trailed by two developing economies: Argentina and Brazil, indicative of the changing configuration in the international division of labour (Table 7.6).

Table 7.6:   UK Exports of Bulk Malt Whisky, 1971 – 9

|  | 1971 | 1975 | 1979 |
|---|---|---|---|
| Japan | 3.4 | 11.7 | 16.5 |
| Spain | – | 0.4 | 2.1 |
| Argentina | 1.9 | 3.6 | 1.6 |
| Brazil | 2.0 | 3.2 | 1.3 |
| Other countries | 1.2 | 1.7 | 2.9 |
| All countries | 8.5 | 20.6 | 24.4 |
| Percentage of total exports | 4.7 | 8.8 | 9.3 |

Source: Compiled from: UK Monopolies and Mergers Commission, *Hiram Walker-Gooderham & Worts Limited and the Highland Distilleries Company Limited: A Report on the Proposed Merger* (London, HMSO, 1980).

Analysis of the global whisky circuit would be incomplete without recognising another vital link in the chain, namely the importer/distributor. Many distributors of distilled spirits are themselves giant multi-commodity traders, and assume prominence in all alcohol sectors where exports are significant. Essentially, the functions of the importer/distributor are largely wholesale, including holding and financing inventories, shaping pricing policies, and promotion of the specific brand. DCL, for example, has contracts with 3,000 distributors in some 200 markets, from Hong Kong's largest trader (Jardine Matheson) in Japan, and Schenley in the USA, to numerous smaller trading companies in the Gulf region.

This trading network, which has evolved over the last two centuries with its very high distributor mark-ups, is now being encroached upon by another group of multi-commodity traders having recourse to what is known as 'parallel trading'. It consists of traders purchasing well-known brands in the UK and shipping them to overseas markets where they underprice the traditional distributor/importer. Those who are potentially best positioned to profit on a large scale from 'parallel trading' are precisely those traders with the most globally sophisticated marketing networks.

It ought not to be obscured that, although the whisky giants dominate UK spirits, there are other formidable corporate agents in other spirits categories. United Rum Merchants, a subsidiary of Booker McConnell, is vertically integrated from sugar plantations to rum distilling and is the dominant force on the UK dark rum market. Likewise, Grand Metropolitan's liquor subsidiary IDV, already encountered in the beer, wine and whisky markets, is important in gin, vodka, rum and liqueurs not only in the UK but in several developed and developing countries as well. IDV ranks a close second after DCL among the largest transnational alcohol TNCs based in the UK, with the corporate roots of its various predecessor firms harking back as early as the seventeenth century (Figure 7.2). Already in the nineteenth century, Gilbeys (now a major IDV subsidiary) developed South Africa into a springboard to build an international empire of wine buying and selling, which today has ramified into IDV's wine and spirits investments in several African countries.[30]

*France*

As against whisky's leading role in the UK, distilled spirits in France are dominated by two completely different sets of beverages: cognac and aniseed-based drinks, with two companies as the clear market leaders. Moët-Hennessy, whose operations as a major champagne producer have already been described, exercises a no less paramount role in global cognac markets, controlling 17 per cent of that market by 1980. With 96 per cent of its aggregate output exported, its future

Figure 7.2: IDV: The Corporate History, 1678 – 1972

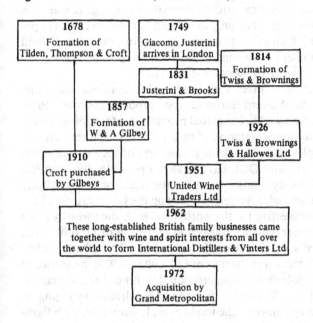

Source: *Impact*, 15 October – 1 November 1980.

in this product is inextricably linked to the consolidation of an expansion in overseas markets. Joined to Martell, Courvoisier and Remy Martin, Moët-Hennessy controls roughly three-quarters of the world wine cognac market. Two of the big four (Martell and Remy Martin) still remain family-owned firms.[31]

Turning to the other giant, Pernod Ricard, one perceives another facet of corporate market structure. Aniseed-based beverages alone comprise a third of French distilled spirits consumption, with Pernod Ricard appropriating 75 per cent of this market. The major variation between the aniseed and cognac markets is that the former is still largely produced for domestic demand. Not surprisingly, therefore, over four-fifths of Pernod Ricard's aniseed sales are in France. In view of a relatively saturated domestic market, it has its sights set on boosting external sales to the levels of its French aniseed sales by the end of the 1980s. This marketing offensive is being led in the USA by its recently acquired Austin Nicols, a major beverage distributor.[32]

A major factor reinforcing Pernod Ricard's expansionist drive is precisely its powerfully entrenched diversified beverage power. It is France's market leader not only in aniseed but also in colas (71 per cent), soda (16), fruit juices (18), fruit drinks (16), calvados (17) and cassis (14); number two in wine-based aperitifs, port and cider; and among the top five in armagnac and cognac.[33]

Such market data reveal very little of the economic war being waged within the Western European geo-corporate complex. Prior to the era of TNCs wedded to global promotional technology, there was only minor interpenetration of national drinks markets. At present, the complex global marketing structures of such corporations as Pernod Ricard and DCL have rendered possible, for example, sustained attacks by whisky firms on the traditional non-whisky French consumer and, inversely, aniseed on the UK consumer. Seen in a broader perspective for the world market, Scotch whisky is the indisputable leader with 7.9 (measured in million of hectolitres) as against aniseed's 1.9. Likewise, Scotch whisky TNCs have broken into the French market to the tune of £50 million (1979) in contrast to aniseed's negligible counter-penetration thus far of the UK market.

The aniseed/whisky battle is but one of hundreds now raging on alcoholic beverage markets the world over. Indubitably, such fighting will intensify as mounting corporate reinforcements are flung into the battle to promote specific alcohol brands in the 1980s.

## The FRG

As the third ranking spirits producer in the Western European geo-corporate complex, the FRG provides a highly suitable terrain for TNC economic onslaughts. Its distilled spirits sector is as relatively fragmented as its beer sector, with no giant companies dominating the sector. Eckes,[34] the distilled spirits market leader, has aggregate sales of only $372 million (1980),[35] and, combined with the next two largest, appropriated less than a quarter of the market. Hence the scope for further domestic concentration[36] and foreign intrusion is potentially tremendous.

A sustained drive to concentration is well underway: whereas spirits sales soared almost fourfold in two decades (1960 – 79), the number of spirits firms plummeted from 415 to 172.[37] To speak of overall concentrated power or its absence, however, partially obscures an overpowering reality: the big three in most spirits categories dominate the commanding heights: in acquavit (84 per cent), brandy (72), herb/bitter liqueur (64), apple-flavoured corn brandy (62), wine brandy (54), vodka (37), whisky (26) and corn brandy (21).[38]

Foreign encroachment is making rapid headway. Of the FRG's top 101 spirits brands, 20 are TNC imports, with 12 emanating from the Anglo-French spirits giants.[39] Another invasion route in its early stages is the setting up of TNC subsidiaries inside the FRG with Seagram as the trail blazer.[40]

## Japan: The Geo-corporate Complex

Moving from the traditionally deeply entrenched European spirits complex to another epicentre of DME power, one perceives a historically novel constellation of forces. As with consumer electronics, automobiles, shipbuilding, and a large swathe of other industries, Japanese distilled spirits are now poised to become major contenders on the global market.

As with almost all the nation's industrial sectors, distilled spirits have attained a high pitch of concentration. One TNC alone — Suntory — depicts the parameters of corporate power, with sales outstripping $4.0 billion (1982). Its corporate tentacles extend into all major spirits categories, comprising over two-thirds of whisky, the major distilled spirit,[41] as well as vineyards in Japan, France and California. The latter is a joint venture with the Firestone rubber company.

Since Suntory's humble beginnings in 1899, its pervasive presence is now seen in all alcoholic beverages, with its power ramifying massively from output into retailing via its 30,000 franchised Suntory pubs. These multi-sectoral strides are being matched by no less prodigious advances in automated technology, seen in their 1973 computerised distillery which generates three-fifths of its aggregate malt whisky requirements with a mere 75 employees. Further, these technical innovations are underpinned by Suntory's own central research institute that pursues research into all major alcoholic beverage categories.

Suntory has conglomerated into soft drinks in a major way, as well as into pharmaceuticals and communications through acquisition of a part of the Tokyo Broadcasting System.[42] It is also heavily involved in food processing and restaurant chains. Since 1979, it has plunged into a number of oil and gas exploration ventures.

From this increasingly diversified domestic base, Suntory has pushed its operations into Asia and beyond. Such expansion is rooted in the thesis that corporate survival on the domestic market requires uninterrupted penetration of the global market — a policy prescription that is increasingly shared by other TNC majors in alcoholic beverages.

Its paramount brands are exported to the world's leading spirits consuming nations, including certain CPEs, and, in several cases, merchandised by Suntory's own restaurant chains.[43] In certain developing economies and CPEs, it has commenced local production via a complex of output and marketing agreements, including the Philippines, Thailand, Mexico, Brazil and Bulgaria.

Already a formidable world corporate power, Suntory, if its recent annexationist trajectory is any indicator, inexorably stands on a major collision course with the North American and Western European geo-corporate complexes.

## Notes

1. The five leading categories are whisky (including Scotch, bourbon, Canadian and blends), gin, vodka, rum and a category which includes brandy and liqueurs.
2. One aspect of the global economic crisis which exercised a discriminatory impact on smaller distillers was spelled out by *Advertising Age* (27 July 1981): 'The woes of the liquor industry's past year were compounded by high interest rates, which raised the cost of storing and aging distilled spirits. Interest rates also prompted retailers to reduce inventory, providing sporadic shortages in certain products.'
3. The vast majority of the multi-commodity traders are private companies. Even for the public corporations, which are compelled by law to disclose a balance sheet, the data are sometimes presented in a manner designed to obscure rather than reveal their mode of operations. Invariably, there is no breakdown of aggregate figures by commodity composition in their annual reports.
4. Seagram and Hiram Walker from Canada; NDCC, Heublein and Brown-Forman of the USA.
5. Seagram holds over 20 per cent of the US distilled spirits and wine market, about double Heublein's share. *Business Week*, 27 April 1981.
6. These are Seagram, Hiram Walker and NDCC (figures for 1975). See Eric Single, 'The Costs and Benefits of Alcohol in Ontario: A Critical Review of the Evidence', paper prepared for conference on 'Economic Aspects of the Use and Misuse of Alcohol', University of Essex, 12–15 November 1981, p. 3.
7. *World Drinks Report*, 31 March 1981.
8. Directly or indirectly, Seagram owns at least 30 distilleries in 19 countries. See Eric Single, 'Intercorporate connections of the alcohol industry in Canada', unpublished essay of the Addiction Research Foundation, Toronto, 1982.
9. Understandably, a member of the top three families, Mr Paul Desmarais, is on Seagram's board of directors. Via his own private holding companies (with assets of *c.* $8 billion), he controls the Power Corporation of Canada whose subsidiaries include mutual funds and trust companies, life insurance, Great Lakes shipping, trucking, newsprint and numerous other enterprises. In the verdict of the *Financial Times*, 'it is

difficult for the ordinary Canadian to exist a week without enriching Mr Desmarais in some way' (*Financial Times*, 4 June 1981).

10. See Peter Newman, *Bronfman Dynasty* (Toronto, 1979); and the same author's work, *The Canadian Establishment* (Toronto, 1975). See also Jorge Niosi, *The Economy of Canada: A Study of Ownership and Control* (Montreal, 1978).

11. Highlighting the impact of this trade, Newman notes: 'Worst of all, between 1920 and 1930, some thirty-four thousand Americans died from alcohol poisoning; two thousand gangsters and five hundred prohibition agents were killed in the many gunfights triggered by the trade's excesses.' (*Bronfman Dynasty*, p. 88.)

12. It owns nine such facilities in the USA, with the biggest having a capacity of 1.2 million bushels of grain. *Fortune*, 19 October 1981.

13. While the total whisky market declined in 1981, a measure of their Brazilian success is evidenced in increased sales of over 40 per cent, notwithstanding a price well above that of its leading competitor.

14. It had been run by the Sandeman family since its setting up in 1790.

15. With due allowance for hyperbole, the rationale behind this deal was articulated by Seagram's *Annual Report* (1981): 'The success of Robert Brown stems not only from its quality but also from the unique strength of the Kirin – Seagram partnership, combining Kirin's reputation, distribution network and knowledge of the Japanese market with Seagram's distilling technology and marketing skill.'

16. *Business Week*, 27 April 1981.

17. CEMP is an acronym for Mr Samuel Bronfman's four children: Charles, Edgar, Minda and Phyllis, who use the holding company as the investment arm of their family trust. It is believed to control assets amounting to over Can.$9 billion. Edper is an abbreviation of Mr Allan Bronfman's two sons, Edward and Peter.

18. The fall-out from this gigantic sale now nets Seagram 1 million dollars daily in interest payments. *Fortune*, 18 May 1981.

19. *Fortune*, 18 May 1981.

20. *Guardian*, 24 March 1981. In a 1978 US Securities and Exchange Commission document, Seagram disclosed that it had been embroiled in illegal payments and questionable practices between 1972 and 1976. It defended its illegal activities on the grounds that such practices are 'widespread in the United States alcoholic beverage industry'. Seagram also pleaded guilty to 43 counts of commercial bribery in West Virginia alone. It paid out a $50,000 fine and four of its executives were fined $12,500.

21. *Forbes*, 30 August 1982.

22. As with Seagram, certain of Hiram Walker's petroleum acquisitions have been heavily underpinned by finance capital. Via large offshore bank loans — an avenue that is blocked off to small companies — this firm bought up almost 1 billion-dollars-worth of US oil and gas properties. According to the *Financial Times* (16 January 1981) 'one aim was to shelter from taxes some of the company's US distilling income' which at that point accounted for 60 per cent of consolidated profits.

23. *Fortune*, 14 June 1982, and *The Economist*, 8 May 1982.

24. Heublein, *Annual Report*, 1981, p. 3.

25. Ibid, p. 15.

26. As the report pointed out, 'Highland has a much greater share of the market than its number of distilleries might suggest, and it appears that Highland with Hiram Walker would be the largest supplier in the new fillings (newly distilled whisky) market.' The Monopolies and Mergers Commission, *Hiram Walker-Gooderham & Worts Limited and the Highland Distilleries Company Limited: A Report on the Proposed Merger* (London, HMSO, 1980), p. 9.

27. DCL employs about half the entire work-force in the Scotch whisky industry. *Financial Times*, 10 February 1983.

28. An admix is a spirit produced by blending in overseas countries bulk malt Scotch whisky with locally produced spirits.

29. A similar movement is visible in the global cognac trade. Bulk cognac shipments accounted for over 11 per cent of global cognac traded, rising to as high as 40 per cent in cognac exports to Japan. As in whisky, Suntory is among the corporate leaders in this practice. *World Drinks Report*, 8 December 1981.

30. *Wine and Spirit*, February 1980.

31. *Newsweek*, 5 July 1982. Martell, the world's largest producer of cognac, has diversified well beyond cognac into perfume, beauty-care products and luxury leather accessories.

32. It was a former Liggett subsidiary. The rest of the Liggett Group was acquired by Grand Metropolitan, after a long takeover battle in May 1980. *Impact*, 15 October – 1 November 1980.

33. Pernod Ricard, *Annual Report*, 1981.

34. Eckes's parent firm is a family enterprise, consisting of a core group of six companies headed by the original firm of Peter Eckes, founded in 1857.

35. Between 1970 and 1977, the big three's market share rose from 19 to 23 per cent. Monopolkommission, *Hauptgutachten*, for the following years: 1973 – 5, 1976 – 7, 1978 – 9 (Baden Baden).

36. There are also domestic policy prescriptions abetting concentration, with three large excise duty increases (from 1976 to 1981) paving the way. The contention of the German spirits industry association (*Bundesverband der Deutschen Spirituosen-industrie*) is that these measures will push medium-sized firms into bankruptcy.

37. *Eurofood*, 5 June 1980.

38. 'Spirituosen: Zahlen, Daten, Trends', *Selbstbedienung Dynamik im Handel*, October 1980.

39. In 1979, France accounted for 43.5 per cent of the FRG's distilled spirits imports, followed by the UK with 18.2 per cent. *Le Moci* 13 October 1980.

40. Seagram has three brands among the FRG top 100. *Eurofood*, 12 June 1980.

41. Whisky constitutes 20 per cent of Japan's entire alcoholic beverage sector. Suntory's share jumped from 64 to 70 per cent of the whisky market from 1978 to 1981. *Brewing and Distilling International*, August 1981.

42. These acquisitions have been reinforced by Suntory's public relations activities, now centralised in a $7.5 million Suntory Foundation designed to instruct non-Japanese into its conception of Japan's political, cultural and economic role in the world economy.

43. In addition to overseas liquor and restaurant interests, in the USA alone, Suntory owns a PepsiCo bottler, a wood product company and shares in a California winery. *Brewing and Distilling International*, August 1980.

# 8 WHOLESALING AND RETAILING

Missing so far in this corporate mosaic have been the mechanisms by which alcohol flows from producers or traders to final consumers. An analysis of distribution networks is a crucial component of the entire methodological departure of this work. Consequently, the book studies the beverages in question in their totality, emphasising the connections of alcohol sectors with others. In so doing, it investigates the output of, and trade in, these commodities by dissecting corporate power at each specific stage of commodity output. Such a dissection of processing, marketing and distribution chains is founded on the tested conviction that it would be erroneous to confine analyses to a single commodity, as the generalised process of global accumulation has led to an interlacing of inter-commodity flows determined by corporate, political, economic and market power.

In many ways, the French wine sector provides an insight into the complexity of certain alcoholic beverage markets as it includes producers, brokers, shipping merchants, merchants specialising in maturing wines, distribution merchants (also designated consignees or bottlers), numerous intermediaries, retail stores, restaurants and cafés. Whereas around half of French wine passes through each of these individual distribution channels, there is an observable tendency towards merging of wholesale and retail functions into single corporate enterprises, labelled the integrated trade.[1] It would appear that this coalescence of functions is the wave of the future for alcoholic beverage sectors the world over.

As against items of clothing, alcoholic beverages have in common with food a retail structure where products are sold not only through take-home outlets, but also via pubs and restaurants. Take-home sales as a per cent of total beer consumption vary widely from country to country in Europe: the UK (12 per cent), the FRG (40), Belgium (50), the Netherlands (60) and Denmark (77).[2]

## Wholesaling

In most countries, the major intermediary between producer and retailer is the wholesaler, a sector also marked by rising concentration in most DMEs. In much of the developing world, no strong nationwide wholesaling network exists, and large producers often distribute their products directly to retailers.

While specific data on alcohol wholesaling are fragmentary in most countries, an indication of its structure can be gleaned from selected examples. In France, where traditionally distribution has been fragmented, one large wholesaler, Générale de Boissons, handles 12 per cent of all beer, mineral water and soft drinks in France, as well as a fifth of bulk dispensers for the hotel, restaurant and café trade.[3] In the USA, there is yet another set of pressures pushing concentration. Legislation that would authorise territorial monopolies in beer distribution (modelled on similar soft drink legislation[4]) is being promoted by the National Beer Wholesalers Association which, if enacted, would swiftly whittle down the 4,500 beer wholesalers. Vertical extensions by the giant brewers into wholesaling operations also abets concentration.[5]

## Retailing

Basically, there are four types of alcohol retail outlets, each with its own specificities, and each varying from country to country:

1. multiple retailers;
2. exclusive alcohol outlets;
3. duty-free shops;
4. social retail outlets.

In all four (save duty-free shops) the march to concentration is conspicuous.

Although alcohol sales are restricted to state-run stores in certain countries, in others the multiple retailers are surging ahead in this sector. Stemming from their massive merchandising turnover, these retailing giants can and do underprice competitors with their own brand labels. This has the dual impact of squeezing both smaller retailers and smaller producers, a classic example of how concentration in one sector can be transmitted to another. Multiple retailer incursions into alcohol are most visible in the UK, headed by Marks & Spencer, Sainsbury, Tesco, Safeway and even British American Tobacco's (BAT) subsidiary International Stores.[6] Notwithstanding historically fragmented retail networks, Italy and France have undergone a similar metamorphosis. Over seven-tenths of Italian alcohol purchases are made through supermarkets, and already by 1984 it is projected that nine-tenths of French wine and spirit sales will be transacted in hypermarkets.[7] One by-product of this shift to multiple retailers, whose major customers are women, is that both producers and retailers are increasingly targeting female consumers.[8]

Another major retail outlet are state and private establishments exclusively selling alcohol. Whereas in certain countries all alcohol flows through these outlets, in others there is a mix in which wine and spirits are distributed through state liquor stores, and beer is available elsewhere. A recent innovation is the emergence of large private owned retailers, often subsidiaries of conglomerates, selling only alcohol. Grand Metropolitan's IDV recently inaugurated what it claims is Europe's first wine superstore, where it merchandises its own brands. It remains to be seen what influence such marketing trajectories will exercise on consumption.

With the explosion of tourism and business travel, duty-free shops have become a major alcohol retail outlet. The genesis of duty-free shops can be traced back to Ireland's Shannon airport in 1949. By 1981, over 250 million travellers spent $5 billion on duty-free goods: 40 per cent on alcohol, 30 per cent on tobacco and 20 per cent on perfume. The bulk of the world's duty-free shops are owned by airlines, ferry operators and airports, while some are rented out to independent operators. Over half such shops are located in Europe (one-tenth in Scandinavia) followed by the Far East with one-third.[9] The price allurements to the world's airline passengers (745 million in 1980) are impressive: the overall average alcohol price differential between French hypermarkets and duty-free shops (1978) was 30 per cent, but soared as high as 59 per cent on gin and 67 per cent on *anisette*.[10]

Restaurants, pubs, cafés and other social retail outlets remain predominantly small scale and labour intensive, notwithstanding the rise in concentration of pubs and restaurant chains in certain countries. Ineluctably, precisely the same forces spurring concentration in other retail sectors will come to operate more conspicuously in this sector.

## Notes

1. At the end of 1979, 45 per cent of French wine passed through the integrated trade. *Revue vinicole internationale*, December 1979.

2. *Financial Times*, 4 March 1981.

3. Générale de Boissons controls a total of 70 beverage wholesalers. *Brewing and Distilling International*, June 1980.

4. See Public Law 96 – 308, 96th Congress, 9 July 1980, 'The Soft Drink Interband Competition Act', 15 USC 3501.

5. Anheuser-Busch has a network of 950 wholesalers, over a fifth of the US total. *Business Week*, 12 July 1982.

6. Despite Sainsbury trailing Marks & Spencer in licensed outlets (192 versus 250), they claimed to have the highest throughput of wine per shelf space in the UK. In 1980, they sold over 200,000 bottles of their own (73) wine brands weekly. *Wine and Spirit*, June 1980.

7. *Market Research Europe*, February 1982, and *Revue vinicole internationale*, January 1980.

8. For certain health implications of this retailing shift, see Dr John Hughes's 'observations' in the *Guardian*, 17 September 1982.

9. *The Economist*, 21 August 1982.

10. *Revue vinicole internationale*, October 1979 and December 1981.

# PART THREE: CORPORATE MARKETING STRATEGIES

# 9 THE MARKETING COMPLEX

In their most rudimentary expression, corporate marketing strategies are designed to separate the consumer from his money. In pursuit of this goal, the modern corporation has built up a series of inter-related professions and techniques to package, advertise, promote and price its products to maximise the dual targets of profit and market aggrandisement. Specific marketing strategies for the major legal addictive products — alcohol and tobacco — are essentially similar to those of TNCs in all other consumer product lines. Because of the addictive nature of these products, however, perceptible nuances are discernible in their promoters' preoccupations with creating a product image imbued with concern for individual health, safety and the sociability of their consumption.

Central to all TNC marketing strategies is the comprehensive integration of each individual component. Nowhere is this more clearly elucidated than in the words of the chairman of the world's largest brewery, Mr August A. Busch III:

> In 1977, we installed a programme which we call 'Total Marketing' which combines all of the key marketing elements into a single orchestrated thrust. Advertising was joined by sales promotion, merchandising, field sales, sales training and sports programming, enabling us to market not only on a national plane, but also at the grass-roots level. This 'in the trenches' capability, coupled with our national programmes, will prove vital to our growth in the eighties.[1]

Increasingly, corporate marketing strategies are adopting both the terminology and techniques of warfare, symptomatic of the underlying, fierce competitive antagonisms unleashed on the global market. The pervasiveness of this approach was underlined in the American *Journal of Business Strategy* that merits quotation at some length:

> The increased need of business to develop competitor-centred strategies to win market share will lead managers to turn more and more to the subject of military science. The classic works of

Clausewitz, Liddell Hart, and other military theorists are being increasingly combed for ideas, just as economic theory and consumer behavior theory were studied in the last two decades.

Business people frequently use military talk to describe their situations. There are price 'wars', 'border clashes', and 'skirmishes' among the major computer manufacturers; an 'escalating arms race' among cigarette manufacturers; 'market invasion' and 'guerilla warfare' in the coffee market. A company's advertising is its 'propaganda arm', its salesmen are its 'shock troops', and its marketing research is its 'intelligence'. There is talk about 'confrontation', 'brinkmanship', 'superweapons', 'reprisals', and 'psychological warfare'.

But the real question is whether the use of 'warfare' language in business is just descriptive or whether it really aids in thinking and planning competitive strategy. We believe it does, and that principles of military strategy apply in three critical business decision areas — namely, determining objectives, developing attack strategies, and developing defense strategies.[2]

The astronomic sums involved in such marketing strategies and, no less so, in the legal takeover wars are such that only the largest can survive.[3]

It is crucial for understanding alcoholic beverage marketing strategies to see them in the context of mounting corporate concentration, transnationalisation, conglomeration and oligopolisation in the beer, wine and distilled spirits sectors, as mapped out in the previous chapter. Had alcoholic beverage sectors remained competitively fragmented, corporate marketing warfare would never have attained its present lethal pitch. With the wine sector as a possible exception in certain countries, national and global marketing warfare among a handful of giants has been revolutionised by the conglomerate intrusions of such battle-tested veterans as Philip Morris and Coca Cola. Tracing the new battle lines of the 1980s, one of Gallo's vice-presidents noted: 'Coke has lots of money and can do whatever it wants.' Similarly, as *Impact*'s editor added: 'Coke said there are no rules, and whatever it takes to build a brand we will commit ourselves to.'[4] Such are the unconditional terms of corporate survival.

Part III is centred on understanding four decisive components of corporate marketing warfare — advertising and promotion, overseas sales strategies, pricing policies and TNC linkages to finance capital.

## Notes

1. *Brewers Digest*, January 1981.
2. Philip Kotler and Ravi Singh, 'Marketing Warfare', *Journal of Business Strategy*, Winter 1981. The interaction of offensive and defensive strategies was exemplified in a takeover battle between General Cinema (the leading independent American soft drink bottler and motion picture exhibitor) and Heublein, which, as the designated takeover victim, counter-attacked with its own takeover bid. The manner in which the war itself was waged is significant. After annexing 10 per cent of Heublein's shares, General Cinema announced its intention to acquire a controlling interest in the company. Heublein launched a counter-attack by counter-annexing 3.5 per cent of General Cinema and threatening to make a tender offer for at least 51 per cent of its outstanding shares. *Business Week*, 22 March 1982; and the *New York Times*, 12 March 1982.
3. As Ralph Nader observed:

The posture of two agencies (the Antitrust Division of the US Justice Department and the Federal Trade Commission), with a combined budget of $20 million and 550 lawyers and economists trying to deal with anticompetitive abuses in a trillion-dollar economy, not to mention an economy where the 200 largest corporations control two-thirds of all manufacturing assets, is truly a charade.

Quoted in M. J. Green, B. C. Moore and B. Wasserstein, *The Closed Enterprise System* (New York, 1972), p. xii. See also M. S. Lewis-Beck, 'Maintaining Economic Competition: The Causes and Consequences of Antitrust', *Journal of Politics*, Vol. 41 (1979). By 1980, 20 US corporations employed over 100 in-house lawyers each (AT & T 902, and Exxon 384). Du Pont allocated 39 corporate lawyers exclusively for antitrust work.
4. Both quoted from *Business Week*, 15 March 1982.

# 10 ADVERTISING AND PROMOTION

## Historical Foundations

Since the last quarter of the nineteenth century, which witnessed the large concentration of industrial and finance capital, advertising and its attendant promotional techniques have been at the epicentre of corporate marketing strategies. Advertising technology, from this historic watershed, evolved in tandem with major innovations in production technology and management techniques. Communication and transportation revolutions, associated with the mass expansion of the telegraph and the railway, swelled the number of daily and weekly newspapers in the USA and Europe after the 1870s. Corporate capital immediately seized on the upsurge in newspapers as an advertising medium that came to complement posters as a visual and psychological device for boosting sales and moulding consumer behaviour.

Alcoholic beverage advertising imparted another major impetus with the onset of the commercial production of industrial glass, notably bottles, that became part of a larger packaging revolution with cardboard boxing a significant component. Large-scale commercial bottling made possible alcohol merchandising via the mail order trade. Even prior to the turn of the century, whisky sales, underpinned by advertising, were available through mail order houses which were some of the precursors of today's large retail establishments.

As distinct from brand identification, which is the quintessence of contemporary advertising, the earliest manifestations of liquor advertising emphasised price as the basic stimulus to consumption. Only during the first decade of the twentieth century were brands destined to assume their psycho-social prominence as the decisive advertising conduit.

While deliberate falsehoods, exaggerated and misleading assertions have been major traits of advertising since its incipience, the earliest forms bordered on what would appear today as quixotic and even grotesque, as the following exerpts would intimate. Unabashedly, an 1899 US advertisement boasted that in Fig Rye, science has produced a whisky which aids digestion instead of retarding, helps the liver to proper action and keeps the kidneys in a state of perfect health. The introduction of the fig neutralizes all of the unpleasant and dangerous effects of those properties which any whisky made from grains alone possesses.

Yet another in 1900 touted the therapeutic and medicinal effects on the insane: 'Woodland Whiskey was adopted July 1, 1899, by the Department of the Interior of the United States for use at the government hospital for the insane, Washington, D.C., on account of its absolute purity and excellent medicinal qualities.'[1]

In subsequent decades, advertising was to shed much of its mendacious posturings to harness the tools of applied science and statistics, psychology and other forms of consumer manipulation. Large-scale corporate advertising now moved in conjunction with the concentration of industrial and financial capital, becoming in its own right one of the major multi-billion dollar industries. The advertising industry's sheer size, with global billings outspacing $120 billion (1981), gives a clue of its all-pervasive power to generate, direct and manipulate consumer demand in all consumer goods industries.

It is at this juncture that one sees the divorce between traditional economic theory and the reality of mass advertising. Just as the contemporary reality of oligopolistic and conglomerate structures have annihilated traditional neo-classical producer theory, mass advertising has likewise undermined traditional consumer theory. This theory imputes to the individual consumer the freedom to maximise his subjective welfare through rational market choices. The impact of advertising, with that of alcoholic beverages being a prominent illustration, indicates the extent to which the notion of 'consumer sovereignty' is singularly inapplicable in an economic universe dominated by oligopolistic institutions.

In the case of alcohol, advertising technology has been a catalyst of consumption, with all its attendant health-related problems, in several areas:

1. multi-billion dollar advertising has launched new alcohol categories and brands, thus stimulating new alcohol tastes;
2. lavishly bankrolled marketing drives have helped alcohol compete much more effectively for the consumer's disposable income, thus also enlarging the alcohol market;
3. specifically segmented advertising campaigns have been targeted

to pull in new consumer groups, e.g. females and adolescents, where alcohol consumption has traditionally been low.

Mass advertising's effectiveness in moulding consumer choice is even more pronounced in most developing countries, where far fewer corporations bombard the consumer and where less effective consumer protection mechanisms exist. Much of this corporate advertising exploits desires by members of the DE elite to emulate western consumption patterns and modes of conduct. This often assumes racist and sexist manifestations, exemplified in San Miguel's Hong Kong advertisements, which feature a mixed group of Chinese males and white females. This approach is explained by San Miguel, 'because we think some Chinese would like western girl friends'.[2]

## The Numbers Dimension

Advertising's all-pervasive influence is glimpsed in clearer perspective through the analytical prism of global advertising billings, which measure the major media outlets: magazines, radio, television, newspapers and outdoor placements. It should be underscored that these figures underestimate total advertising outlays as they exclude other promotional devices, including the sponsorship of sports events. As can be expected, there are huge variations between countries in the volume of resources deployed in advertising, ranging from an estimated 0.04 per cent of GNP in Ethiopia to over 2 per cent in the USA.[3]

Indeed, the USA has appropriated fully one half of global advertising expenditures. Together with the next five epicentres of corporate power, Japan, the FRG, the UK, France and Canada, they account for around four-fifths of the total.[4]

Global alcoholic beverage advertising surpassed $2.2 billion in 1982, an estimated 1.6 per cent of global advertising. Once again, an estimated half of this sum was spent in the USA, which placed the brunt of the alcohol advertising onslaught on the American consumer (Table 10.1). A strong US movement towards deregulating government codes and restrictions on corporate practices in the early 1980s can be expected to accentuate further the avalanche of consumer advertising. Under the constant pressures of deregulation, the National Association of Broadcasters dismantled its advertising code in 1982, which had prohibited distilled spirits advertising and restrained the volume of advertising minutes per television hour. With the formal code gone, the floodgates are open to expand an already huge $2.6 billion prime time television advertising outlay.[5]

Table 10.1:   Advertising Expenditures[a], 1979 – 81 ($ billion)

| | 1979 | 1980 | 1981[b] |
|---|---|---|---|
| Total advertising expenditures | | | |
| World | 96.8 | 108.0 | 120.4 |
| USA | 49.8 | 54.0[c] | 61.3 |
| Alcoholic beverage advertising | | | |
| World[d] | 1.62 | 1.80 | 1.94 |
| USA | .86 | .90 | .97 |

Notes: a. Based on 'measured' media: magazines, radio, television, newspapers and outdoor placements.
 b. Estimates based on global advertising growth rate of 11.5 per cent in 1980.
 c. Estimates based on USA totalling half of global expenditures.
 d. Estimates based on global advertising totals being double US totals.

Source: *Impact, Advertising Age*, various issues; *Economist*, 20 September 1980; *International Herald Tribune*, 11 June 1980.

It is precisely due to the central position of the USA in global advertising that most of the analytical illustrations used are drawn from US advertising techniques. While beer and spirits are the clear leaders in US alcohol advertising, nonetheless wine is the fastest growing of the three: wine advertising outlays leaped almost three-fold per gallon in the 1970s.[6]

One of the major factors inhibiting new corporate entrants into the alcohol industry has been the prohibitive cost incurred by the leading TNCs on major brands. This is but one more glaring factor contributing to corporate concentration away from the atomistically competitive markets of traditional theory. Over $20 million was spent on each of the five leading beer brands and the leading wine brand in 1980, and over $10 million each on another twelve alcoholic beverage brands.[7] A major contributory factor in these drives were the incursions of the conglomerates Philip Morris and Coca Cola into the US beer and wine markets. Even wine market leader Gallo had been surpassed in 1981 by Coca Cola's $30 million advertising avalanche, which compelled all their major competitors to escalate sharply their advertising outlays. Seven of the top 100 advertisers in the USA are major alcoholic beverage producers, with combined measured advertising outlays (excluding their substantial international outlays) outstripping $1.1 billion (Table 10.2).

Table 10.2:   US TNCs Producing Alcoholic Beverages: National Advertising Expenditures, 1980[a] ($ million)

| National rank | Company | Advertising expenditures | Sales |
|---|---|---|---|
| 4 | Philip Morris | 364.6 | 9,822.3 |
| 20 | Coca Cola | 184.2 | 5,912.6 |
| 21 | Anheuser-Busch | 181.3 | 3,295.4 |
| 26 | Heublein | 170.0 | 1,974.8 |
| 30 | Seagram | 152.0 | 1,588.2 |
| 71 | Schlitz | 66.4 | 896.7 |
| 72 | Brown-Forman | 65.0 | 468.3 |
| Total | | 1,183.5 | 23,958.3 |

Note: a. Excludes international advertising.
Source: Computed from trade sources.

A more coherent perspective of the magnitude of alcohol advertising is gleaned from an investigation of specific media outlets. In magazine advertising, for example, alcoholic beverages exceed tobacco as the leading advertiser with well over 10 per cent of total billings. Seagram and Philip Morris are both among the top four magazine advertisers. In the outdoor advertising category, tobacco was the clear leader with about one-fifth of total billings, trailed by alcoholic beverages in second place with about one-tenth.[8] In this respect, the USA is representative of the ad profile in most DMEs.

**The Drive to Market Segmentation**

In view of the heterogeneity of consumers in all societies by sex, age and ethnic, income and geographical groups, TNCs in all consumer product lines have attempted to expand markets through product differentiation and brand proliferation. Another factor which corporations consider in their brand creation is the incidence of national cohesion in the market. In the UK beer market, where local and regional identities are still tenacious, Allied-Lyons has spawned a brand portfolio of about 50 beers. In contrast, the US beer industry generates a far more cohesive national market, in which Philip Morris has deployed a market strategy rooted in merely four brands.

Underlying the strategy of segmentation are highly sophisticated and prodigiously financed marketing surveys, which have identified those markets most vulnerable to corporate penetration. The major segmentation criteria in launching new brands are highlighted in the following examples.

## Female Recruitment

As women swelled the ranks of the DME labour forces in the 1960s and 1970s, paralleled by powerful social movements calling for greater female emancipation and participation, corporate power moved to cash in on this socio-economic upsurge. By the late 1970s, these social dynamics were joined to recessionary economic forces that depressed male consumption in several countries. One specific form this assumed was the corporate targeting of women as a rising consumer group worthy of special attention. This has involved two kinds of corporate strategy applicable to all forms of market segmentation: generating new brands and retargeting older ones. Seagram's £1.75 million promotional campaign for a new brand in 1980 was sanctified as follows: 'Crocodillo is the first completely new drink to be developed out of consumer research specifically for young women during the last decade.'[9]

Retargeting is exemplified by Brown-Forman's push to reposition their leading whisky brand, Jack Daniels, towards women. 'As the brand has gotten bigger,' notes an executive from Brown-Forman's advertising agency,

> we have kept looking for places to find new drinkers . . . Vodka has done all right with women, but women are a big, untapped category for whisky. We felt there was a potential, especially with upscale working women, and particularly with working women who make their own brand decisions.[10]

Consequently, Jack Daniels became one of the first distilled spirits brands to run advertisements in leading women's magazines. Seen in a wider context, it is not only the alcohol TNCs that are pushing their advertisements on women's magazines, but the magazines themselves, due to escalating costs and their dependence on advertising revenues, which are also blatantly soliciting the alcohol TNCs.[11] Thus, the overall advertising avalanche is by no means exclusively the brain-child of the alcohol TNCs, but rather the resultant of a self-reinforcing network that meshes TNCs with the media.

Alcohol corporations are attempting to win over women not only through targeted advertising and new brands but also through campaigns at the retail level. Pubs and taverns tied to alcohol companies in the UK have launched massive campaigns to improve facilities for women and children. To take but one example, Grand Metropolitan has invested £25 million in attracting women to its Chef and Brewer pubs through such techniques as 'free flower week', in which all female customers are greeted with flowers. Other techniques include offering women chocolates at a discount, a ladies' happy hour, a mother's day special and a Valentine-night scheme. In short, no avenues for increasing female consumption of alcohol have remained unexplored.

*Corralling Youth*

While women's importance as a consuming segment is unparalleled in size, the youth market assumes paramount importance for yet another reason. Because of legal prescriptions against alcohol sales to adolescents in most DMEs, alcohol advertising TNCs can hone in on the entry level age-group to recruit consumers at a formative age. To make further deep forays into this segment, TNCs often strive to reshape certain existing brands so as to enhance their youth appeal. By recourse to commercials depicting the attractiveness of dangerous and exciting occupations, Philip Morris has moved in on this market.[12] Similarly, Grand Metropolitan claimed to have discerned through a market survey that their gin products were being purchased by an ageing consumer group, which it attempted to counteract by launching a novel cartoon advertising campaign for its Gilbey's brand aimed at the youth market.[13]

Another conduit to the youth market has been massive promotion on college campuses via such gimmicks as sponsorship of concerts and beer parties. In the words of the *Washington Post*, this 'is nothing more than a well-calculated and minor business risk: invest a little money today to gain a lot back tomorrow', a view confirmed by a salesman of Philip Morris's Miller Beer: 'We lose money in college marketing. We are into short run losses and hopefully long run gains. We are trying to create brand awareness.'[14]

*Ethnic Pursuits*

In most countries, there exist substantial culturally differentiated ethnic minorities. The potential of these segments has not yet been fully realised by corporate advertising capital, although once again the US advertising giants have been pioneers in this field. Brewer market surveys have provided fairly accurate breakdowns of the urban centres where black consumer markets are concentrated so that specific brands can be targeted. What appears to be valid for beer is no less so for wine and distilled spirits.[15]

## Income Strata

As with a staggering array of firms producing consumer durables and non-durables, alcohol TNCs often create brands corresponding to the disposable income of specific social classes. This comprises 'popular' brands priced to attract lower income groups; 'premium' brands aimed at higher income groups; and 'super-premium' brands directed towards the summit of the income pyramid. Such brand differentiation can be misleading inasmuch as it often involves little more than affixing different labels on bottles of essentially the same product. As alcohol corporations switch their marketing acumen to developing countries, particularly in distilled spirits, they invariably place less emphasis on popular brands due to the inability of the vast majority living in poverty to purchase commercial distilled spirits.[16]

## Locational Patterns

Geographic segmentation can and does play an important role in countries where entrenched traditional local and regional loyalties still exist. Whereas in the USA and Japan corporate concentration, coupled to highly unified transportation and communications networks, has contributed largely to eradicate such regional loyalties, in the UK and the FRG these loyalties continue to exercise an impact on consumer choice. Thus, the latter two's leading brewers have retained a staggering variety of local and regional brands. Or, as the *Financial Times* puts it for the UK market: 'Regional names for beers and local pricing arrangements are the order of the day at the large brewery companies.'[17] Such entrenched regional loyalties have no parallels in developing countries due to the relatively short history of their commercial alcohol consumption, which permits the easier penetration of single national brands.

## Competitive Substitutability

Because distilled spirits comprise several competitive categories, corporate capital often creates different brands within a given category (e.g. rum or whisky), each with a specific competitive capability. Illustrative is Bacardi's grand design on the US market, where it has launched five specific rum brands each aimed at a different spirits category:

1. silver rum, to compete with vodka and gin;
2. amber rum, to compete with American whisky;
3. 'Gold Reserve', to compete with brandies;
4. '1873', to compete with Scotch whisky; and
5. 151 proof rum, for use in mixed drinks or in cooking.

A similar corporate marketing vision also looms in the wine horizon with Villa Banfi's positioning of its Riunite brand: 'Today we consider any liquid at all our competitor. We are positioning ourselves like a soft drink.'[18] This is one of the revolutionary changes of the 1980s that demarcates it from previous decades.

*Light versus Heavy Consumption*

Perhaps the most recent innovation in market segmentation techniques has been the brand differentiation between heavier and lighter drinkers. While most marketing energies have been directed towards the lighter end of the drinking spectrum, certain specific beer brands have been aimed at the heavier end, such as Philip Morris's malt liquor destined for the consumer who drinks 18 – 24 bottles per week.[19] Conversely, a focus on the less heavy alcohol consumer emerged in the mid-1970s with the appearance of beer with 20 – 35 per cent fewer calories and lower alcohol content, billed as 'light' beer. This shift to 'light' beer exhibits similarities with the innovations of low tar cigarettes and sugarless soft drinks, and often involves the same TNCs (e.g. Philip Morris and Coca Cola). These innovations were largely responses to concerted social pressures from consumer, health and government agencies which centred on health-related problems.

For the world's two biggest brewers — Anheuser-Busch and Philip Morris — their massive entry into, and subsequent dominance of, the light beer market has offered an unparalleled bonanza, as the segment has proved recession-proof. Their marketing success stems in part from their appeal to the health- and weight-conscious female beer consumer, as well as their no less deliberate pursuit of the male market by recourse to sports personalities and the sporting cult in their promotional efforts. Such low alcohol beer has already made inroads in certain other DMEs, notably Australia, where it has gouged out a tenth of the national beer market. In most developing countries, where weight consciousness is not a primary concern, this species of product differentiation is of minor consequence.

It was only a matter of time before success in light beer would exert a demonstration effect on the wine sector.[20] It is not fortuitous that Coca Cola, with its vast marketing know-how in low sugar/calories soft drinks, would herald the innovation of a light wine with lower sugar and alcohol content.[21] Whereas, prior to 1980, California state law required that all wine should contain at least 10 per cent alcohol, removal of this restrictive measure has not only unleashed a wine war in this segment, but is fundamentally reshaping wine production and consumption patterns. With this deregulative measure, the flood-gates were opened for other giants (notable Heublein, Schlitz, Norton Simon and Seagram) to plunge into the fray with unprecedented advertising sums.[22] Such legislative manoeuvring of output standards runs along the same track as the earlier noted deregulation of advertising, in that both are contributing to blaze new marketing vistas for corporate power.

## Emergence of New Alcohol Categories

While the above categories of market segmentation define the parameters of corporate criteria in shaping new brands, it must not be surmised that these delineate the exclusive and formal boundaries of corporate choice. Rather, in the limitless quest to annex new markets, novel alcohol categories are being created. A prominent illustration of such a prime mover is Grand Metropolitan's creation (through its IDV subsidiary) of the cream liqueur category designed primarily to hit the female market. Cream liqueur is a creation of chemical technology, which has spawned one of the fastest growing alcohol categories world-wide, triggering a market chain reaction of new TNC intruders.[23]

## Generic Advertising

Discussion in the eight preceding subsections can by no means be considered an exhaustive treatment of advertising techniques. Whereas these subsections have delineated the various strands of brand advertising, there exists, albeit on a far lesser scale, what could be designated as another advertising subset that transcends specific brands and deals with alcohol categories in their totality: generics.

The word genus, from which is derived the adjective and noun 'generic', originally refered to a category of biological classifications comprising related organisms, usually consisting of several species. Translated into corporate nomenclature, species become brands, and generic categories are specific product lines, for example cigarettes, wine, beer, etc. In certain DMEs, a growing amount of food products are being retailed under plain generic labels, which in the case of the USA scales 12 per cent. Already generic labels have appropriated 3 – 5 per cent of the US wine market and are making inroads into distilled spirits.[24]

The purchasing rationale behind 'generics' is price. Inasmuch as the 'generic' product has not been subject to advertising expenses, it sells for as little as half the price of its equivalent brand.[25] From the perspective of corporate merchandising, the rationale behind producing such 'generics' is the attempt to capture that segment of the market that has developed, as it were, antibodies against, and hence immunity to, advertising.

Another manifestation 'generics' assume, this time bankrolled by advertising, is state-supported export programmes for entire product lines. In each of the three major world alcohol export sectors — UK Scotch whisky, French wine and French spirits — the state and trade associations have buttressed export drives with major advertising campaigns for specific alcohol categories as a whole.[26]

## Importer Link-ups

Producers, governments and trade associations are not the exclusive advertising agents on the global market. Rather, when alcoholic beverages are exported, another economic agent assumes the advertising burden: the importer/distributor.

In view of the complexity and diversity of various global markets, alcoholic beverage producers often find it lucrative to delegate advertising in foreign markets to economic agents endowed with a far more intimate merchandising expertise in that specific market. Invariably, the importer/distributor (at times a subsidiary of the corporation) takes over the advertising function. Nonetheless, decisions concerning the amount of advertising money to be spent in each market remain with the TNC producer. While the distributor/importer is expendable if it fails to meet corporate sales expectations, this form of corporate linkage often survives years of close intermeshing. Staggering sums are often involved, seen in $6.5 million deployed by Grand Metropolitan to its US importer, Austin Nicols, to promote the Bailey's Irish Cream brand.[27]

**The Advertising Phalanx**

Such a discussion on advertising would be incomplete without an analysis of the dominant corporations that engineer such advertising.

The giant advertising corporations that consolidate the $120 billion global advertising phalanx have become an indispensable adjunct of corporations in all economic sectors, of which alcohol is but one important component. Led by Japan's Dentsu and the US giants Young & Rubicam and J. Walter Thompson, twelve globe-straddling advertising agencies (each with yearly billings over $1 billion) jointly appropriate over 17 per cent of global billings.[28] It is precisely these large advertising companies that acquire the bulk of contracts awarded by the biggest alcohol corporations. Their marketing expertise encompasses a wide range of consumer product lines, not least that of another addictive product — cigarettes.

As with alcohol TNCs themselves, the marketing leverage of several of the leading advertising agencies is bolstered by their conglomerate reach. Within a short time span, Young & Rubicam annexed 15 corporations to become a leader in such related fields as public relations, package design, sales promotion, direct marketing and advertising to specialised professional groups.[29] Annexation of other corporations to form a more coherent corporate galaxy is but one strategy. Another, no less effective, one is the build up of joint ventures between the largest advertising agencies to penetrate further a given market. Dentsu and Young & Rubicam already have a joint venture in Japan and similar hook-ups are on the corporate drawing board for other global markets.[30] Nor are TNC advertisers immune to annexation, seen in Saatchi & Saatchi's 1982 takeover ($57 million) of US advertiser Compton, which propelled the combined agencies into one of the world's top ten advertisers.[31]

It is vital for understanding the mechanisms and networks of the global market that precisely the same big twelve advertising agencies are omnipresent in both the developed and developing countries. Shifting the focus to the five largest Latin American markets, for example, J. Walter Thompson is the major advertising agency in Argentina, Chile and Venezeula; number two in Brazil and number four in Mexico.[32] Thus, precisely the same marketing technology perfected in the developed economies is adaptively deployed to promote alcoholic beverages and other product lines in the developing countries. Indeed, given their vast economic intelligence networks, in many cases they command a more sophisticated mastery of consumer behaviour in local and national markets than most governments.

### Parameters of the Debate

However incredulous it may appear, given the billions of dollars that nourish alcohol advertising, there is an important current of opinion (partially fed by corporate capital) which contends that these colossal advertising sums exercise no impact on pulling new consumers into the alcohol vortex. Or, in the rationalisation of SAB, 'advertising . . . cannot cause movement in overall consumption'.[33]

In both tobacco and alcohol, the two major legal addictive substances, the debate on advertising's impact has acquired universal dimensions, stretching from the USA to Papua New Guinea. Conventionally, advertising's protagonists have insisted that their campaigns are not geared to escalate consumption, but rather to encourage those who already drink to switch to a particular brand. Counterpoising this argument are those who attribute increased alcohol consumption by young age-groups, women, individuals in developing countries and other social categories to sustained publicity onslaughts that glamorise alcohol and vaunt its consumption as a prescription for problem solving and success in business, social encounters, sports and sex.[34]

A myriad of ostensibly 'scientific' research monographs has grappled with the relationship of advertising to consumption in several countries. This book is not concerned with fuelling the debate with statistical series for or against; but rather with indicating the fallacious foundations of the debate. Above all, the source of funding of these studies must be carefully scrutinised, since in several cases it is the alcohol power network (at times through their trade associations) that directly or indirectly bankroll these monographs. It should come as no surprise that what was touted as a distinguished study, whose austere conclusions were 'that no scientific evidence exists that beverage alcohol advertising has any significant impact on alcohol abuse', was sponsored and funded by the US Brewers Association.[35]

Such a plethora of partisan studies tends to obfuscate the issues and generate a debate which is largely motivated by, and is in the interests of, the alcohol power complex. Why, it may be asked, should alcohol and tobacco advertisements differ from ads of other products which are blatantly endeavouring to raise both market shares and consumption? Indeed, it is wholly irrelevant how TNCs construe their advertising intentions, inasmuch as both their textual and visual brand imagery is non-discriminatory in its permanent cerebral bombardment of both adults and adolescents, males and females, blacks and whites and, above all, drinkers and non-drinkers.

Another dimension of the debate's misleading parameters is that it is centred exclusively on advertising, and hence any policy prescriptions emanating from it tend to focus exclusively on advertising. Given, however, the previous analysis and what follows, such a narrow debating vision obscures the evolving totality of alcohol TNCs' promotional strategies which reach well beyond the formal confines of advertising.

## The Permanent Transformation of Consumer Awareness

In their quest for the permanent revolutionising of consumer awareness, alcohol TNCs are transforming the technology of marketing persuasion. Faced with various impediments (e.g. advertising bans), the TNC, like water confronting a rock, merely flows around it, deploying its prodigious resources by other techniques. Thus, it would be fallacious to infer that a specific institutional ban would exert any more than a marginal deterrent impact on TNC marketing. Some of the salient interrelated techniques of the alcohol TNCs' constantly evolving marketing apparatus are depicted below.

*Free Sampling.* A technique deployed through various retail outlets where brand awareness is refurbished and/or generated by the free distribution of the product. Pernod Ricard has experimented widely with this technique in pubs, clubs and discos, targeted to a youth audience.

*Supporters Clubs.* Creation of clubs by specific TNCs where members are entitled to buy a range of memorabilia touting the brand. Guinness launched its supporters club in 1981 in 13,000 pubs in the UK and Ireland, drawing in 55,000 members.[36]

*Promotional Tours.* Essentially deployed by wineries to attract tourists via free sampling and factory tours. Around two million tourists yearly visit California's Napa Valley wineries as a result of this technique.[37]

*Sports and Leisure Promotion.* In certain cases, entire corporate departments have been scaffolded to research sporting and leisure interests of alcohol consumers, aimed at corporate sponsorship of specific athletic events. Anheuser-Busch has become the dominant sponsor of sporting events in the USA, and probably in the world, totalling 98 professional and 310 college sporting events in 1981.[38]

*Logo Merchandising.* A technique whereby alcohol TNCs contract clothing manufacturers to produce items bearing the corporation's brand. Depending on the nature of the market, this merchandise is sold slightly above cost, below cost or distributed freely, and represents a highly effective device for proliferating brand awareness, strikingly so in developing countries.

*Telephone Delivery Services.* A relatively new technique, innovated by Seagram, that facilitates merchandising, as consumers can place toll-free telephone orders for delivery of the company's brand, with payment by credit card. Such levels of merchandising sophistication are only feasible for those giant TNCs with far-flung national distribution networks and are thus beyond the reach of smaller companies.

*Treasure Trove Gimmickry.* This genre of generating brand awareness involves concealing cases of alcohol in certain areas, and then purchasing media outlets to give clues as to where the alcohol 'treasure' may be found. Hiram Walker has disbursed as much as $10 million on what it bills as a 'Hide-a-case' campaign in Canada's wilderness.[39]

*Taste Test Competition.* This involves the purchase of prime time television during major sporting events for a live competition between drinkers to select the better of two brands. Schlitz has poured $4 million into this technique to challenge its two leading competitors.[40]

*Targeting Retail Outlets.* Essentially this consists of directing resources towards those retail outlets where alcohol consumption has hitherto been non-existent or restricted. These include fast food outlets, sport stadiums, convenience stores, airlines, etc. Targeting such outlets is being abetted by technical innovations in packaging engineered for specific outlets. Light, compact aluminium cans (for wine retailing in airlines) and large bag-in-box containers (for dispensing wine in restaurants) have been among Coca Cola's leading innovations.

*Shelf-space Manipulation.* While shelf positioning has long been a retailing strategy, it is only within the last decade that it has acquired its highly sophisticated forms. This technique is based on marketing surveys and computerised shelf alignment studies which seek to uncover the psychology of product location *vis-à-vis* other product lines, geared to maximise sales. Manuals elaborating such scientific techniques are distributed by Gallo and other alcoholic TNCs to retailers.

*Point of Sale Promotion.* With kinship to supporters' clubs, alcohol TNCs often provide distribution outlets with a wide array of free point-of-sale consumer items, bearing their logo, as well as discount coupons. Deregulation, at least in the USA, is facilitating the propagation of this technique by giving freer rein to instore product displays.[41]

While these interrelated techniques are generally deployed by individual corporations, there are cases where promotion can be executed through joint corporate efforts. California's wine grape growers have proposed the setting up of a 'co-ordinating commission' that would, in their perspective, direct 'consumer education' (i.e. moulding consumer behaviour to the service of corporate goals) for its wines.

The reverberations of these combined sales, advertising and marketing techniques are being felt not only in DMEs, but in certain DEs, as the ongoing Philippine beer war highlights. Philippine *per capita* beer consumption is still relatively low by international standards — 14 litres versus 146 in the FRG in 1980. This disparity indicates just how high the stakes have risen. San Miguel, the Philippines' fourth largest corporation, has enjoyed a virtually unchallenged monopoly for over nine decades. In 1981, a tobacco, banking, construction, chemical and agri-business conglomerate, bankrolled by indigenous and foreign Chinese capital, mounted the attack.

Both are deploying their non-alcohol product lines to cross-subsidise the colossal outlays required to finance the war. According to a San Miguel spokesman, it tripled its beer advertising expenditures merely in one year, concentrating on TV in the urban areas, and radio in the provinces.[42] Compounding the war has been the precipitous drop in rural incomes related to declining raw material prices in the midst of global economic crisis. To forestall a shift by its poor consumers to low-priced indigenous spirits, one of the contenders has introduced a relatively cheap, high alcohol-content brand. The public health implications are that the war is being fought to get consumers more inebriated more quickly at a lower price.

All of the preceding advertising and promotional techniques are orchestrated primarily within domestic markets. With the growing internationalisation of output, trade and capital flows, however, they in turn have been internationalised to underpin the propagation of alcohol the world over.

## Notes

1. Both quoted from *Advertising Age*, 27 July 1981.
2. *Asiaweek*, 23 July 1982.
3. Starch Inra Hooper, *A Survey of World Advertising Expenditures in 1977* (New York, 1979), p. 11; and J. Walter Thompson Co., *Trends in Total Advertising Expenditure in 25 Countries, 1970 – 1979* (London, 1980), pp. 3 – 4.
4. The USA's global share dropped from 54 per cent in 1977 to 51 per cent in 1979. Hooper, p. 5; and *International Herald Tribune*, 11 June 1980.
5. Spelling out the implications of deregulation, one executive noted:

> The temptation to increase the commercial load on hit shows could be irresistible. Why not add an extra minute on a strong programme when you can charge $250,000 for it? There are all sorts of games to play . . . and people will play them because there will be no one to stop it. It would be hard to resist. (*Business Week*, 29 March 1982.)

If such deregulation opens up the television universe to distilled spirits advertisements, the big producers will be ready to exploit this opportunity to expand their marketing vistas beyond the printed media, much of which has an exiguous readership in the poorer urban centres and ghettos.
6. In 1979, US beer advertising hit $370 million; distilled spirits, $355 million; and wine $137 million. It is expected to double by 1985. *Impact*, 15 May 1980. In a US Federal Trade Commission survey using 1975 data, distilled spirits ranked fifth out of 214 product groups in media advertising as a per cent of sales. *Advertising Age*, 19 October 1981.
7. Over $40 million each was spent by Anheuser-Busch and Philip Morris on their leading beer brands. *Beverage World*, June 1981.
8. Tobacco and alcohol, the two major legal, addictive consumer product lines, account for about a fifth of magazine advertising and about a third of outdoor

advertising. See *Advertising Age*, 3 March 1980, and 13 July 1981; and *The Bottom Line on Alcohol in Society*, Spring 1981.

9. *Wine and Spirit*, October 1980.

10. *Advertising Age*, 27 July 1981.

11. *Family Circle*, a leading US women's magazine, vaunted itself in *Advertising Age* (27 July 1981) to alcohol TNC executives with the following attributes: American women make up 48 per cent of the alcoholic beverage market; of the 16 million women that read *Family Circle*, over 10 million are between the ages of 18 and 49, and nearly 9 million are employed, equalling one-quarter of all working women in the USA; and buyers of *Family Circle* select all or some of the alcoholic beverage brands in four out of five households. See also *Houston Chronicle*, 21 February 1982.

12. *Advertising Age*, 16 February 1981.

13. *Wine and Spirit*, March 1980. Not to be outdone, Bacardi is focusing on younger drinkers through a joint campaign for mixed drinks with Coca Cola. 'We should now be able, with the cocktail promotion, to hold people longer in age terms,' contends Bacardi's chairman. *The Times*, 10 June 1982.

14. *Washington Post*, 9 October 1983.

15. Villa Banfi market researchers concluded that blacks are likely to constitute a major market for wine in the 1980s. Hence the inundation of black publications with ads such as one featuring Miss Black America of 1980 touting their Riunite brand. *Advertising Age*, 27 July 1981.

16. For illustrations of this strategy, see 1981 annual reports of Heublein and Seagram.

17. *Financial Times*, 5 March 1982.

18. Quoted from a Villa Banfi executive. *Business Week*, 15 March 1982.

19. *Advertising Age*, 9 February 1981.

20. Another technological spin-off of light wine and beer was the advent of non-alcoholic grape-based and malt-based beverages, which are making inroads into those regions where alcohol consumption has been discouraged or banned for cultural/religious reasons. As with light beers and wines, it is precisely the giant TNCs that are taking the lead in this form of market segmentation.

21. Light wines are produced by a combination of two methods: harvesting the grapes early when their sugar content is low, and passing the wine through a vacuum distillation process to burn off some of the alcohol.

22. In 1981, Seagram launched its biggest wine campaign to date, involving an $18 million outlay for its own light wine. *Advertising Age*, 20 July 1981.

23. For the moment Grand Metropolitan, through its Bailey's Irish Cream brand, dominates 80 – 90 per cent of the global market, which has been growing at 35 per cent yearly. *Wine and Spirit*, November 1981.

24. *New York Times*, 5 July 1981.

25. Illustrative of these price differentials is a generic Scotch whisky which retails in the USA for less than $4, as against the $9 J & B brand. *New York Times*, 5 July 1981.

26. 'The problems of Scotch whisky in the crucial US market', according to the *Financial Times* (10 October 1981), 'were highlighted recently by the decision of the Scotch Whisky Association — the industry's trade body — to launch a $1.5 million three year campaign to make consumers in the US more aware of the virtues of Scotch — the first generic campaign of this kind that the Scotch makers have indulged in.'

27. *Wine and Spirit*, August 1981.

28. These include: Dentsu (1980 global billings: $2.7 billion); Young & Rubicam ($2.2 billion); J. Walter Thompson ($2.1 billion); McCann-Erickson ($1.7 billion); Ogilvy & Mather; Ted Bates; BBDO; Leo Burnett Co; SSC & B; Foote, Cone & Belding; D'Arcy-MacManus & Masius; and Doyle Dane Bernbach. *Advertising Age*, 20 April 1981.

29. For a glimpse of Young & Rubicam's annexationist strategy, see *Wall Street Journal*, 2 March 1982. The significance of the conglomerate intermeshings were spelt out:

> The companies that were acquired tapped into Y & R's capital, administrative and computer support, its influence in buying ad space and its global string of offices. They also got access to Y & R's roster of blue chip clients . . . Y & R opened doors to Procter & Gamble Co., General Foods, Merrill Lynch and others.

30. Dentsu has already appropriated around a quarter of Japan's advertising billings. *Financial Times*, 4 June 1981.

31. *Advertising Age*, 22 March 1982. One motive behind this merger was that the two agencies shared ten TNC clients, including Procter & Gamble, IBM, Du Pont and Nestlé.

32. *Advertising Age*, 25 May 1981. Malaysia's three leading beer brands are all promoted by TNC advertisers: Guinness by Ted Bates, Carlsberg by Leo Burnett, and Anchor by McCann-Erickson. *The Star* (Malaysia), 29 June 1982. In Thailand, TNC advertisers have propelled alcohol into the fourth leading advertising product (1981) after home appliances, watches and soap. *Bangkok Post*, Special Supplement on Advertising, 22 March 1982.

33. *The Journal* (Toronto), 1 March 1982.

34. The debate attained such levels of controversy in the USA, that the Senate deemed it worthy of extensive hearings in 1976 and 1977. See United States Senate, *Hearings on Media Images of Alcohol and the Effects of Advertising and Other Media on Alcohol Abuse*, before the Subcommittee on Alcoholism and Narcotics, Committee of Labor and Public Welfare, 8 – 11 March 1976; and United States Senate, *Hearings on Alcohol and Drug Abuse among Young People*, before the Subcommittee on Alcoholism and Narcotics, Committee of Labor and Public Welfare, 24 – 25 March 1977.

35. See *Modern Brewery Age*, January 1979.

36. *Financial Times*, 1 October 1981.

37. *Advertising Age*, 18 May 1981.

38. *Business Week*, 12 July 1982. Moctezuma, one of Mexico's big three brewers, has sponsored such diverse athletic and gastronomic events as 'a pie-eating contest, hairy legs competition, ballon stomp, tug o'war in the mud, dunk tank competition, trivia contests, tricycle race, egg toss, and of course, a beer chugging relay race' (*Modern Brewery Age*, 13 August 1979).

39. *Wall Street Journal*, 23 July 1981.

40. *Advertising Age*, 19 January 1981.

41. For US Treasury Department reforms, see *Beverage World*, March 1981.

42. Interview with one of San Miguel's vice-presidents, 27 July 1982.

# 11 OVERSEAS SALES STRATEGIES

## An Overview

The rationale of the overseas drive stems from a multiplicity of factors. During the early colonial period, rum and molasses, as by-products of the cane-sugar industry, became an important commodity in international trade. This was in part due to the need for a payment medium in the triangular slave trade, and in part a result of demand in regions bereft of the primary raw material input. One of the constants stimulating international trade in alcoholic beverage since the mercantilist period of the seventeenth century has been the reality that, despite the risks, higher margins could often be earned in overseas markets.

This was one of the major reasons behind the international marketing of alcoholic beverages. Because of a deceleration of population growth since the 1960s, certain national markets reached the upper limits of consumption. As from the early 1970s, this was coupled with rising raw materials and petroleum costs which spurred TNCs to export as well as extend their operations abroad to continue growing and to slash unit costs.

Breaking into the world market, however, has certain imperatives as competition heightens. Growth on the global market is predicated on a multiplicity of factors that only the biggest have at their command: far-reaching economic intelligence networks joined to distribution facilities, close links with the transnational banking circuit, etc. Export achievement is also tied to close links with large importing companies whose corporate affinities lie with the largest alcoholic beverage companies. Collaboration with certain members of both the public and private sector elite in DEs is yet another important connection in TNCs' overseas implantations. Grand Metropolitan's joint venture with the governments of Malawi and Kenya to produce wine and spirits is descriptive of this movement.

It should not be surmised that such massive TNC incursions would remain unchallenged either by certain governments or by the organised labour movement. Invoking the infant industry protectionist thesis of the nineteenth century, Fiji's prime minister justified protectionism for a new rum plant on the grounds that the multinationals who have been selling these commodities in our country chose to dump their products on our market in order to strangle this new industry. This indicates that if we do not give protection to a new industry, we will never be able to establish any manufacturing industry at all.[1]

Another challenge of a different order came from workers in one of Papua New Guinea's TNC breweries, who called on the government to nationalise the country's two beer corporations 'because these two breweries are making huge profits and the profits are going out of the country to a small number of shareholders, which doesn't represent real development for Papua New Guinea'.[2] Noteworthy is that opposition to TNCs in these cases stems not from public health considerations, but from certain interpretations of national economic interests.

To illuminate the nature and mechanisms of these relationships, subsequent sections study four major techniques of internationalisation: exports, subsidiaries and joint ventures, licensing agreements and barter.[3]

## Exports

All the major alcoholic beverages are exported, but their incidence varies from region to region and from beverage to beverage.

### Beer

Stemming from the relative ease in setting up breweries abroad and beer's relatively low unit costs, exports are much less important for beer than for wine and spirits. Nonetheless, beer exports are a global reality, in particular towards DEs where beer consumption is rapidly growing and to certain CPEs, notably the swiftly growing Chinese market. Other motivating elements behind beer exports have been the continuous recent and forecasted beer stagnation in many DMEs, as well as the imperatives of earning foreign exchange, even in CPEs. A notable cross-current of the 1980s, however, is that certain DEs are speeding up import substitution industrialisation policies, with breweries often high on the priority list.

Global beer exports are under the control of a relatively small number of giant TNCs, led by the quasi-monopolistic corporations designated as Group C in previous chapters: Heineken, United

Breweries and Guinness. To these traditional global market pace-setters will be added in the 1980s the leading TNCs from Groups A and B. As pungently articulated by an Anheuser-Busch executive:

> Less than one per cent of our total volume presently is sold internationally — and the world beer market is four times larger than that of the US. Moreover, our research tells us, as the world comes closer together in a travel and communications sense, tastes change too. We think that will augur well on a long term basis for American malt beverages, and we are taking steps now to be in a position to take advantage of such opportunities.[4]

Already, it is precisely Anheuser-Busch, together with the traditional three, that top the list of beer imports into the burgeoning Japanese market.[5]

While beer exports will undoubtedly escalate competition on the world market, there is yet an element of corporate co-operation which coexists with such competition. This takes the form of TNC brewers directing exports to foreign markets via the intermediary of a TNC importer, which in many cases happens to be another brewer. Anheuser-Busch has opted to break into the French market through a hook-up with France's leading brewer, BSN Gervais Danone, and has followed a similar path into Japan via Suntory. In certain cases, imported brands can be deployed to beat back other foreign brands imported by a corporate competitor. Oetker, the FRG's number three brewer, sought to import Anheuser-Busch's Michelob brand to fight back Tchibo/Reemtsma's Tuborg import in the super premium price range. Thus competition, nationally or globally, can in no way be considered incompatible with certain forms of corporate co-operation.

## Wine

Due basically to the specificities of soil and climate, most wine is marketed internationally through exports. Indeed, by the late 1970s, the value of wine export was four to five times greater than that of beer. Unlike beer, wine is not consumed by the lower income groups in most DEs, and hence the major export markets are found in North America, Western Europe and Japan.

As distinct from beer, where only the largest firms hit the world market, both medium- and large-size wineries in southern Europe have traditionally dominated the global wine market. Striking mutations are already underway, however, in the 1980s. Giving this new offensive its tone and substance are the giant conglomerates that are taking over the US wine market, which are mobilising their vast resources to enter other markets. Here again, the pre-condition for success is finding connections with the giant importers/distributors, whose corporate sectoral roots differ from one country to another. Leading among these in the USA are subsidiaries of the giant beverage companies: Brown-Forman, Heublein, PepsiCo and Moët-Hennessy. In the UK, wine subsidiaries of the giant brewers lead the pack. In Japan, it is the Sogo Shoshas (general trading companies) with their extensive trading networks.

## Distilled Spirits

Even more so than wine, most distilled spirits are largely consumed by higher income groups, and hence the major traditional markets continue to be the DMEs. Within the DMEs, however, there have been discernible shifts with import growth decelerating in the United States and accelerating in Japan.

An inquiry into one of the world's largest alcohol trading routes, namely Japanese imports of whisky, reveals that it is the giant TNCs and traders which effectively control global distilled spirits markets. DCL has staked out one-half of the Japanese whisky import market, followed by the corporate giants Hiram Walker (7.6 per cent) and Seagram (3.4 per cent), both spanning several whisky categories.[6] Likewise, among the importers/distributors, several Japanese Sogo Shoshas are prominent, as well as the leading Hong Kong trader, Jardine Matheson, importer of three DCL brands (Table 11.1).

In specific markets, spirits TNCs at times utilise a notable variation to their collaborative relationship with importers/distributors. In potentially large markets, where the political climate is considered congenial to corporate capital, TNC producers may at times choose to buy out or set up their own import subsidiaries. Pernod Ricard's 1980 acquisition of the huge drinks distributor Austin Nichols from the Liggett Group is illustrative. By this acquisition it immediately broadened its marketing empire by 240 US wholesalers and retailers that had been meticulously built up over the previous three decades.

Spawning import subsidiaries is by no means incompatible with continuing link-ups with independent importers/distributors. Indeed, DCL ships a segment of its exports to Japan through such independent companies as Jardine Matheson and Suntory, while

Table 11.1:   Japan's Whisky Imports: Major Producers and Distributors/Importers, 1980[a] (per cent)

| | Scotch | Irish | Canadian | American | Total |
|---|---|---|---|---|---|
| Producer | | | | | |
| DCL | 52.1 | — | — | — | 49.9 |
| Hiram Walker | 7.4 | — | 38.8 | — | 7.6 |
| Seagram | 3.3 | — | 6.8 | 3.3 | 3.4 |
| Arthur Bell | 2.9 | — | — | — | 2.8 |
| William Grant | 1.8 | — | — | — | 1.7 |
| Brown-Forman | — | — | — | 45.8 | 1.4 |
| Schenley | — | — | 4.4 | 23.8 | 0.7 |
| Standard Brands | — | — | 38.3 | — | 0.4 |
| NDCC | — | — | 8.2 | 7.7 | 0.3 |
| Others | 32.5 | 100.0[b] | 3.5 | 19.4 | 31.8 |
| Total | 100.0 | 100.0 | 100.0 | 100.0 | 100.0 |
| Distributor/Importer | | | | | |
| Jardine Matheson | 22.1 | — | — | — | 21.2 |
| Caldbeck | 16.1 | 52.6 | — | — | 15.5 |
| Suntory | 5.1 | — | 38.8 | 69.2 | 7.3 |
| Meiji-Ya | 5.4 | 21.1 | — | — | 5.2 |
| Mitsui | 5.1 | 26.3 | — | — | 4.9 |
| Kirin-Seagram | 3.2 | — | 6.8 | 3.3 | 3.2 |
| Marubeni | 1.4 | — | — | — | 1.4 |
| Others | 41.6 | — | 54.4 | 27.5 | 41.2 |
| Total | 100.0 | 100.0 | 100.0 | 100.0 | 100.0 |

Notes: a.  First half of the year.
   b.  100 per cent produced by Irish Distillers.
Source: Computed from data in *Shokuhin Sangyo Shinbun*.

another segment is imported via its own subsidiary, Old Parr, thus diminishing the risks associated with each of the two trading options.

**Subsidiaries and Joint Ventures**

Although exports have been over several centuries the major medium for the conquest of external markets, it was only after the Second World War that the establishment of subsidiaries and joint ventures became a major corporate overseas strategy. A major motivation in setting up overseas subsidiaries is to bypass the myriad of tariff and non-tariff barriers that affect exports. For distilled spirits alone, the UK National Economic Development Office

(NEDO) identifies 17 types of barriers in numerous countries (Table 11.2). Over time, the scaffolding of subsidiaries came to assume one of two corporate forms: marketing subsidiaries of the kind seen in Austin Nichols or Old Parr, and production subsidiaries. By the very fact that they are subsidiaries linked to parent firms, the possibility for transfer pricing prevails.

Table 11.2:    Distilled Spirits: Tariff and Non-tariff Barriers, 1981

| Type of barrier | Markets | |
|---|---|---|
| 1 Total ban (on other than religious grounds) | Brazil Jamaica Albania | India Bolivia Guyana Fiji |
| 2 Part ban | El Salvador | |
| 3 State monopolies | Iceland Norway Sweden Finland Turkey Kenya Canada USSR Hungary Yugoslavia Albania Poland Bulgaria Czechoslovakia | East Germany Western Samoa American Samoa Egypt Ethiopia Angola Mozambique Tanzania Syria Rumania Zambia Taiwan S. Korea Cuba |
| 4 Exchange control | Sudan Nigeria Turkey Argentina Nicaragua Ecuador Colombia Costa Rica Jamaica Dominican Rep. | E. Europe Paraguay Zaire Ghana Ethiopia Morocco Gambia Sierra Leone S. Africa |
| 5 Licences | Portugal Kenya Greece Uruguay Colombia New Zealand Nicaragua | E. Europe Peru Ecuador Nigeria Ghana S. Africa |
| 6 Duty discrimination | Denmark France | Puerto Rico Philippines |

|    |                            |              |                 |
|----|----------------------------|--------------|-----------------|
|    |                            | Venezuela    | Spain           |
|    |                            | Italy        |                 |
| 7  | Credit restrictions        | Argentina    |                 |
|    |                            | Greece       |                 |
| 8  | Import surcharges          | Costa Rica   |                 |
| 9  | Import deposits            | Italy        | Ecuador         |
|    |                            | Costa Rica   | Greece          |
| 10 | Registration of brands     | Guatemala    | Honduras        |
|    |                            | Nicaragua    | Indonesia       |
| 11 | Registration of importer   | S. Korea     |                 |
| 12 | Strip stamps               | Spain        | Dominican Rep.  |
|    |                            | Greece       | Canary Islands  |
|    |                            | Ivory Coast  | Puerto Rico     |
|    |                            | USA          | Philippines     |
|    |                            | Italy        | Venezuela       |
|    |                            | Jordan       | Belgium         |
| 13 | Labels—customs stamps      | Niger        | Ivory Coast     |
|    |                            | Senegal      |                 |
| 14 | Advertising restrictions   | France       | French W. Indies |
|    |                            | Finland      | French Guyana   |
|    |                            | Sweden       | New Zealand     |
|    |                            | Spain        | E. Europe       |
|    |                            | Switzerland  | Egypt           |
|    |                            | Norway       | Middle East     |
|    |                            | Iceland      | Mexico          |
|    |                            | Venezuela    | Ivory Coast     |
|    |                            | Costa Rica   | Sudan           |
|    |                            | Chile        | Aden            |
|    |                            | Tahiti       | New Guinea      |
| 15 | Resale restrictions        | Belgium      |                 |
|    |                            | Greece       |                 |
| 16 | Credit on duty payments    | Eire         |                 |
| 17 | Miscellaneous red tape     | Ivory Coast  | Nigeria         |
|    |                            | Ghana        | Tanzania        |
|    |                            | Kenya        | Zaire           |

Source: NEDO, *Distilling: Gin and Vodka* (London, 1982), p. 11.

Joint ventures, which differ from wholly owned subsidiaries in that equity is shared in various proportions between a TNC and a national public or private sector entity, are largely an economic response to a changing political configuration in the post-independence developing world. For the first time, developing country elites were pulled into a relationship with TNCs which, despite joint equity participation, did not always generate equal benefits to both sides. Over the past two decades, joint ventures have also proliferated in DMEs and CPEs.

Such corporate techniques of overseas expansion have at times been mislabelled as capital exports. While some of the capital deployed in joint ventures emanates from the corporation's internal resources, a much larger share generally originates from sources external to the corporation. These include massive loans from transnational banks as well as local capital siphoned off the market where the subsidiary or joint venture is being set up. Thus, it is often scarce domestic savings in developing countries, and not so-called 'capital exports', which finance the setting up of breweries and distilleries.

One decisive corporate consideration in the choice of setting up a subsidiary in a specific market, rather than exporting to it, is the circumvention of such impediments as tariff and non-tariff barriers. The realm for gain in setting up subsidiaries is vastly extended if the recipient country is a member of a common market complex, thus offering the potential for tariff free exports to a wider economic region.

Nigeria presents a case study of a country drawn into the alcoholic beverage corporate web through joint ventures and subsidiaries on a scale of unprecedented magnitude in both developing and developed countries. Since Nigeria's 1978 ban on alcoholic beverage imports, several of the world's biggest brewers have implanted joint ventures. There are two major inferences than can be drawn from this relationship between TNCs and one of the world's largest developing countries. In almost every case, the TNCs' equity participation is under 50 per cent — 25 per cent for Guinness, and 15 per cent for BSN Gervais Danone. No less disproportionate is the technological component of these ventures, with almost all machinery, equipment and expertise of TNC origin. Replicated on perhaps a smaller scale in many other developing countries, this relationship is designed to perpetuate a state of permanent dependency.

As with beer, wine and distilled spirits TNCs have recourse to joint ventures and subsidiaries, albeit on a considerably smaller scale because of the essentially far narrower markets that prevail for their product lines in most developing countries. In certain large market-orientated DEs, for example Brazil, subsidiaries and joint ventures have been set up to exploit those markets where wine and/or spirit drinking elites exist.[7] In certain DMEs, such joint ventures have become more conspicuous in recent years, seen in French wine ventures in the USA and vice versa. To which could be added the prominent example of Australia, where TNCs (e.g. Philip Morris and South Africa's Rembrand) are playing an ever larger role in wine.

As is to be expected, the domestic counterpart in several of these DE joint ventures are leading individuals or families that are at the apex of the social, financial and industrial pyramid, with concomitant political connections. Understandably, Seagram sought out such attributes in a Thai joint venture producing distilled spirits, with its Tejapaiboon family partner extensively involved in alcoholic beverages, other economic activities and banking.[8]

## Scope and Significance of Licensing Agreements

Another medium whereby TNCs can generate overseas brand recognition and sales, other than through exports or the setting up of plants, is through licensing agreements, deployed increasingly by brewing and distilling TNCs. A license may be defined as a contractual agreement between two firms to produce certain specific products over a specified time period in specified markets. Patents, trademarks (or brands) and 'know-how' constitute the internationally recognised categories of what is commonly designated as 'intellectual property rights' that define the boundaries of technology.

A patent is definable as a limited monopoly conferred by national law to make, use or sell an invention within a national boundary.[9] A trademark or brand is a word or logo adopted and used by a manufacturer to differentiate its products from those of its competitors; or, in the case of a service brand name (e.g. Intercontinental and Pam Am), to differentiate services.[10] Know-how, in contrast to the preceding two, comprises trade secrets, unpatented manufacturing techniques and other proprietary industrial and commercial processes.[11] The corporate *raison d'être* behind licensing is that it opens new possibilities for a TNC licensor to exploit the earnings potential of its brands and expertise in previously uncharted markets.

Amongst the major gains accruing to the TNC licensor is that the bulk of licensing agreements require that the licensee finance an advertising campaign to boost the brand's image, tantamount to deploying its own resources for polishing the long-term image, not for itself but for the TNC. Other gains redounding to the TNC licensor include royalties based on brand sales, as well as a guaranteed market for the sale of certain intermediate products to the licensee.[12] A no less important benefit to be gained by TNC licensors is that, if their brand acquires an important market segment, they are positioned when contractual renegotiations come up to shift the proportionality of gains further in their favour. Such potential forms of TNC pressure (although not always actualised) inhere in all such contractual agreements, but are invariably stronger against developing country licensees than those in DMEs which, in many cases, are themselves TNCs.

There are certain specific constellations of market forces where licensing agreements enjoy the balance of advantage over subsidiaries and joint ventures. During a time of stagnation or a slippage in sales, instead of reporting losses from its subsidiary on its consolidated income statement, the TNC merely receives fewer royalties on its licence. In areas of greater political turbulence and uncertainty, a licence embodies a lesser potential risk than a subsidiary.

Brewers, and to a lesser extent distillers, have led the alcoholic beverage industry in the use of this technique. Heineken and United Breweries have been in the *avant garde* of licensing, each having extensive licensing agreements in developed, developing and centrally planned economies. In certain countries, TNC licensors have acquired up to 10 per cent of the total market, seen in Miller's share of the Canadian beer market through its licensing agreement with Carling O'Keefe. Licensing agreements between such giants as Anheuser-Busch and Suntory, Kirin and Heineken contribute to reinforce the tight control of national markets by TNCs.

A variation to penetration via licensing agreements — in an entirely different political context — was heralded by what has been labelled an open-ended technical assistance agreement between United Breweries and the People's Republic of China. This includes substantial training of Chinese technicians in United Breweries' Hong Kong subsidiary as a step towards modernising brewing techniques claimed to be four decades out of date.[13]

**Barter Agreements**

Barter arrangements between TNCs and CPEs are another avenue for breaking into CPE markets. These arrangements have acquired prominence in the alcohol field over the last decade. One of the major factors that has stimulated barter between TNCs and CPEs has been the latter's desire to curb foreign exchange expenditure wherever possible. Symptomatic, and in many ways typical, of the offensive was the 1972 deal between PepsiCo and the Soviet Government covering Pepsi Cola and vodka.[14]

A by-product of this CPE – TNC deal was its contribution to enhanced concentration in the US alcoholic beverage industry. In anticipation of the deal, PepsiCo annexed (at a cost of $26 million) the sole US distributor (Monsieur Henri Wines) of the USSR's premier vodka, Stolichnaya. Bankrolled by PepsiCo's multi-million dollar advertising, sales of the high-priced vodka outstripped all forecasts, acquiring 65 – 75 per cent of the de luxe vodka market by 1979.[15] In yet another way the deal elucidates the mechanisms by which a TNC can circumvent certain restrictionist policies. With the imposition of a partial US trade embargo on the USSR in 1980, PepsiCo concentrate exports to the USSR were in no way imperilled as they were supplied by its Irish subsidiary.[16]

The Pernod Ricard – USSR deal is indicative of the movement in the 1980s. In exchange for marketing Pernod Ricard's alcoholic and non-alcoholic beverages in the USSR, this French TNC contracted to market Soviet vodka not only within France, but through its African marketing network as well. As foreign exchange restrictions and constraints continue to bedevil global trade, it would appear that such barter agreements could acquire greater prominence, not only in CPEs, but possibly in developing countries as well.

Whereas the preceding sections analysed both domestic and international sales strategies, it will be seen that TNC pricing policies are one of the unifying strands in corporate strategies.

## Notes

1. *Pacific Islands Monthly*, February 1982.
2. *The Globe*, February 1975.
3. An international marketing stratagem outside these four is collaborative agreements whereby a given TNC markets a foreign TNC's brand through its own national network. Pointers in this direction are marketing link-ups between Allied-Lyons and Anheuser-Busch; Grand Metropolitan and San Miguel, etc.
4. The executive also commented on Anheuser-Busch's rationale for choosing Sweden to break into European markets: 'There's a very definite pro-American feeling in Sweden and we're cashing in on it.' (*Advertising Age*, 27 July 1981.)
5. Heineken tops the list with a quarter of the import market, followed by Anheuser-Busch, United Breweries and Guinness. *Brewing and Distilling International*, June 1980.
6. Indicative of such corporate export concentration are French cognac exports to

Japan with Remy Martin, alone, accounting for half of these, a dominance that bears similarity to that of DCL in whisky. Remy Martin is trailed by four brands (Hennessy, Camus, Courvoisier and Martell), which jointly have another 36 per cent of the market. In other words, the top five brands command well over four-fifths of Japanese imports. *World Drinks Report*, 8 December 1981.

7. Even a CPE, China, is involved in such joint ventures. Remy Martin signed a joint venture with the Chinese town of Tientsin to produce wine for the Chinese and export markets. *World Drinks Report*, 23 September 1980.

8. *Brewing and Distilling International*, September 1981.

9.
Relevant concerns relating to patent licensing strategy include the difficulty that potential competitors have in avoiding or designing around the patent or groups of related patents owned by the patentee, as well as the commercial significance of the exclusivity obtained by the patent monopoly. On the other hand, third parties can inhibit the patentee with patents of their own on some similar aspect of the technology. Patent licenses may be granted on an exclusive or nonexclusive basis and, being based on monopolies, can also be circumscribed in various ways to reflect legitimate strategies of the patentee or other market realities.

Quoted in Business International Corporation, *International Licensing: Opportunities and Challenges in Worldwide Technology Management* (New York, 1977) pp. 20 – 1.

10.
Trademark licenses, like those for patents, may be granted on an exclusive or nonexclusive basis. Since the licensee is selling products under the trademark of the licensor, their quality must be acceptable to the licensor. Consequently, stringent quality controls are often imposed on the licensee. Indeed, these are required by the trademark licensing laws of many countries. Such restrictions enhance the licensor's ability to remain close to the licensee's operations. Trademark licenses offer another advantage if managed properly: they can expand the good name of the licensor in the marketplace.

Quoted from ibid., p. 21.

11. Know-how may
constitute a separate body of information, or be ancillary to the workings of a patent. It may include such tangible objects as manuals for materials specifications or operation instructions, formulae, quality-control procedures, patterns, drawings and blueprints, organization charts, plant layouts, performance records, cost-control procedures and training know-how. Marketing expertise and packaging methods usually acquired after substantial investments of time and money are prime elements of a proprietor's know-how. Intangibles such as laboratory practice, sampling techniques and the availability of consultants with experienced engineers, technicians and professional advisors, acting on behalf of the operator, also fall within the concept of valuable, and therefore licensable, know-how. Basic to the property right of know-how is the fact that the corpus of information is not readily available to unauthorized third parties.

Quoted from Robert Goldscheider, 'A Pragmatic View of International Industrial Licensing', *Current Trends in Domestic and International Licensing 1976* (New York, 1976), p. 30.

12. For an elaboration, see UNCTAD, *The Role of Trade Marks in Developing Countries* (New York), chapter 4.

13. *Brewing and Distilling International*, February 1982.

14. Soviet dollar purchases of Pepsi were pegged to PepsiCo's dollar purchases of

vodka, with payments settled on a five-year basis. For an elaboration, see Charles Levinson, *Vodka – Cola* (London, 1978); and J. C. Louis and H. Yazijian, *The Cola Wars* (New York, 1980).

15. *Wine and Spirit*, March 1980.

16. By 1980, PepsiCo's concentrate exports from Ireland to the USSR amounted to 339 tons, valued at 3.4 million roubles. USSR Ministry of Foreign Trade, *Foreign Trade Statistics – 1980* (Moscow, 1981).

# 12 PRICING AND FINANCE CAPITAL

## Pricing Theory

According to the neo-classical paradigm, prices in a purely competitive milieu are shaped and ultimately determined by what could best be described in a simple equation: price equals processed and unprocessed materials costs, labour costs, overheads, miscellaneous expenditures, plus profit. In such an idealised competitive economy, prices will tend to be pushed down to a level where the profit component approaches zero.

Within an uninhibited competitive market this theory is internally consistent. Even in the heyday of economic liberalism in the UK during the 1840s, 1850s and 1860s, however, such idealised conditions did not exist. Rather, unequal power relationships characterised trade, finance and industry. Since the advent of the great depression of the 1870s, not a single sector in any of the DMEs (and more recently in the DEs) has escaped the grip of concentration — not least the alcoholic beverage sector. This has been partnered by new pricing strategies and formulae that bear no relationship to the idealised competitive model.

## Oligopolistic Pricing

As Chairman of the Board of General Motors, and one of the former leaders of American industry, Alfred P. Sloan formulated a model of oligopolistic pricing policy in the 1920s, which remains applicable to the contemporary corporate world. This model quickly became the core of the management and pricing system in General Motors, subsequently extended to the US automobile industry. In this model, the industry leader (in most cases the corporation with the largest market share) sets a price that it believes will provide a desired long-run target rate of return at a given production level. Smaller firms are expected to fall into line with identical prices, with deviant firms subject to considerable pressure to conform from the industry as a whole.

In the most general economic sense, pricing under conditions of oligopoly or duopoly may be defined as a conjuncture in which large corporations act as 'price makers', as opposed to that of unbridled competition, where the individual enterprise is a 'price taker'. The oligopolist fixes a price, then produces and sells at that price whatever quantity the market will take. It is for this reason that price in an oligopolistic industry is sometimes referred to as an 'administered price', or a 'political price'. The essence is that the price is seller determined, with the goal of maximising market shares and profits of the oligopolistic firms.

Despite variations due to different historical and legal contexts, oligopolistic pricing relies on one basic practice, namely price leadership, which 'exists when the price at which most of the units in an industry offer to sell is determined by adopting the price announced by one of their number'.[1]

Price leadership implies not only that pricing policies must be co-ordinated, but also that the price, once agreed upon, must be sustained by the parties to the agreement until a further change is required by the oligopolists collectively.[2] In cases where one firm stands far above the others in the industry in terms of assets, revenues and overall market leverage, such as Kirin and Suntory in Japan, Heineken in the Netherlands and Seagram in North America, price leadership is most evident. Other firms in a given oligopoly accept prices set by the leader inasmuch as these prices are generally profitable, and because they are cognisant of the self-destructive nature of price warfare in which the less powerful stand to lose either their market share or their very existence. When no single firm clearly dominates the arena, price leadership takes on varying forms. In the cigarette, chemical and US beer industry, for example, the leading firms often vie for leadership in initiating price changes.[3]

## Applied Pricing Strategies

In the alcoholic beverage sector, oligopolistic pricing assumes differing specificities according to the morphology of different markets. While TNCs tend to price their products in conformity with what they believe the market will bear, such an approach in no way applies that prices are higher in richer DMEs than in lower income DEs. Since distilled spirits corporations, in particular, direct their DE marketing efforts at the elite, prices charged within DEs are often higher than those in DMEs.

Illustrative is that out of six different Scotch whisky categories exported to a widely different set of markets, there is a variation of up to 247 per cent between the highest and lowest average export price charged for each category.[4] In four of these whisky categories, the highest export prices were on bottles destined for DEs: South Korea, Namibia and Paraguay. The upshot of this is that prices under these oligopolistic conditions have ceased to bear any significant relationship to costs. Rather, market power becomes one of the prime determinants of price. In certain cases, this takes on a blatantly collusive character as in the reported 20 per cent increase in Malaysian beer prices: 'The three local breweries — Guinness, Malayan Brewery and Carlsberg — decided at a meeting yesterday that the new prices would come into immediate effect.'[5]

Another variant of oligopolistic pricing, related to the principle of charging what the market will bear, is the creation of brands targeted to different income groups within a market. Heublein provides a prime example by marketing basically the same quality vodka in both a popular low-priced brand (Popov) and a higher-priced premium brand (Smirnoff).[6] Seagram, another market leader, has imparted yet another marketing twist to pricing formulas by linking periodic price boosts to similar increases in advertising designed to retain brand loyalties. Yet other TNCs have recourse to another marketing practice which involves specifying prices to retailers by supplying 'recommended' price lists. Certain firms enforce such prices by refusing to supply retailers whose prices diverge from the 'recommended' ones. Two major alcohol TNCs have been accused of these practices on the Brazilian market by a major consumer association.[7]

These formulas of oligopolistic pricing are not fixed in time and space. In periods of sharp economic downturn, however, such pricing stratagems are susceptible to rapid change and, in certain cases, to disintegration.

**Price Wars**

With the onset of the global economic recession from the late 1970s, price leadership revealed the symptoms of cracking up in several alcoholic beverage markets. The Franco-Italian wine war exemplifies some of the characteristics of a price war which highlights certain of the conflicting economic forces with their attendant political overtones. The French grape growers protested that Italian wineries were dumping wine on French markets at prices below costs. Further, they contended that French importers were appropriating substantial shares of the marketing gains from their Italian imports.

For their part, the French firms that import cheaper Italian wine and blend it with French wine, counter that the logic of the marketplace compels them to pursue this marketing path, or succumb to their competitors who continue to import and blend cheaper Italian wine. Such a practice is by no means unique to the wine industry, but is also deployed by TNCs in other product lines involving blending (e.g. tea, coffee, textiles, etc.) and by retailers whose merchandise is imported from countries with differing cost structures.[8] Compounding the complexities of this economic war is the fact that certain major French importers also happen to be vineyard owners in Italy. Alone, the Comptoir Agricole Français controls about 5 – 6 per cent of Italian wine imports into France and is also a major vineyard owner in Sicily.[9]

At times price wars reach enormous proportions. In 1983, for example, Gallo began offering wholesalers a 25 per cent discount on a $16 jug of wine. While Gallo's four major competitors were able to match discount pricing of such magnitude, many smaller wineries found it difficult to do so. Hence price cutting, designed to boost consumption, became an engine for accelerating corporate concentration.

Price leadership can also buckle under when TNCs compete for a rapidly expanding retail outlet. When large UK supermarket chains moved into alcohol retailing on a big scale at the beginning of the 1980s, the big six UK brewers unleashed a price war over the limited shelf space, with large discounts to retailers becoming a common marketing practice. In turn, this level of competition degenerated into such cut-throat forms that the brewers' trade organisation deemed it necessary to issue what it labelled 'a code of conduct' on bribes and other manifestations of skulduggery.[10]

## Transfer Pricing

Whereas the foregoing pricing techniques are the emanations of specific market structures, there are other pricing techniques which are made possible by the vertically integrated structures of certain TNCs.

A largely unexplored wellspring of profit maximisation for the alcoholic beverage TNCs (as for all TNCs) is the widespread technique of transfer pricing. This concept, used by the practitioners of corporate accountancy, refers to prices assigned by TNCs to the transfer of goods, services, technology or loans between their related enterprises in different geographical locations. These prices diverge considerably and are distinct from the prices transacted between autonomous corporations. Such a pricing strategy is designed to maximise profits not necessarily for the individual units of the corporation, but for the corporation as a whole.

Divergent national tax structures provide ideal opportunities for enhancing profits through transfer pricing. Inasmuch as TNCs are principally interested in after-tax earnings, they can minimise tax payments by manipulating prices of intra-corporation transactions in a way engineered to shift profits from countries with higher tax rates to those with lower rates.[11]

Since as much as one-third to two-fifths of global trade is conducted between TNC affiliates, the scope for transfer pricing gains are considerable. In the USA, where considerable transfer pricing data exist, almost half of both exports and imports are within the realm of intra-firm trade. For the biggest alcoholic beverage TNCs, whose breweries, distilleries and wineries span the globe, the realm for maximising gains through transfer pricing is enormous.

## Links with Finance Capital

Pricing techniques (as with advertising and promotion) are vital components of the corporate marketing engine. Yet, the full potential of these techniques would never be realised without the close meshing of alcoholic beverage TNCs and the institutions of finance capital.

There are two agencies through which TNBs underpin or are related to alcoholic beverage TNCs: bank ownership of their equity and massive bank loans to TNCs that facilitate mergers and acquisitions.[12]

Banking laws in several countries authorise banks to hold equity in industrial corporations. Traditionally, what has been designated as the universal banking system in the FRG, and which harks back to the nineteenth century, is perhaps the highest global expression of this industrial and banking relationship. No legal difference exists in the FRG between credit, business and equity dealings and, unlike the system in the USA, there are no legal restraints on the banks to gain a foothold in industry. The Federal Cartel Office found that the credit banking sector (i.e. the commercial banks) supplied between 50 – 66 per cent of credit to all manufacturing sectors by the mid-1970s.

Despite the relative fragmentation of the German beer industry, it remains one of the banks' most heavily penetrated sectors, and certainly one of the most complex, as seen in Table 12.1. There are several banks with equity holdings in breweries, led by the

### Table 12.1: FRG: Bank Ownership of Breweries, 1981

| | | |
|---|---|---:|
| 1. | Bayerische Hypotheken- und Wechselbank, AG München | per cent |
| | 1.1     Reichelbräu AG | over 25 |
| |     1.1.1     Sandlerbräu, AG | 100 |
| 2. | Dresdner Bank, AG | |
| | 2.1     Dortmunder Union — Schultheiss Brauerei, Dortmund[a] | over 25 |
| |     2.1.1     Dortmunder Ritterbrauerei, AG | 96 |
| |     2.1.2     Dortmunder Union Brauerei, AG | 100 |
| |     2.1.3     Dortmunder Union Frankfurter Brauhaus, GmbH | 100 |
| |     2.1.4     Bergische Löwenbrauereien | 88 |
| |     2.1.5     Brauerei Iserlohn | 100 |
| |     2.1.6     Brauerei Schlösser | 100 |
| |     2.1.7     Elbschloss Brauerei, AG | 58 |
| |        2.1.7.1     Einbecker | 75 |
| |     2.1.8     Engelhardt-Brauerei, AG | 78 |
| |     2.1.9     Germania-Brauerei F. Dieninghoff, GmbH | 100 |
| |     2.1.10    Kurfürsten-Bräu, AG | 99 |
| |     2.1.11    Schlegel-Brauerei, GmbH | 100 |
| |     2.1.12    Schlossquellbrauerei, AG | 79 |
| |     2.1.13    Schultheiss-Brauerei, AG, Berlin | 100 |
| 3. | Bayerische Vereinsbank | |
| | 3.1     Aktienbrauerei Kaufbeuren, AG | over 50 |
| |     3.1.1     Lammbrauerei, AG | 98 |
| | 3.2     Hasenbräu, AG | over 75 |
| 4. | Vereins- und Westbank, AG | over 25 |
| | 4.1     Holsten-Brauerei, AG | over 25 |
| |     4.1.1     Kaiser-Brauerei, AG | 100 |
| |        4.1.1.1     Beck & Co. Brauerei | n.a. |
| |           4.1.1.1.1     Haake-Beck Brauerei, AG | over 75 |
| |     4.1.2     Bill-Brauerei, AG | 100 |
| |     4.1.3     Brauerei Feldschlösschen, AG | over 50 |
| |     4.1.4     Lüneburger Kronen-brauerei, AG | 100 |
| 5. | Bankhaus Merck, Fink & Co. | |
| | 5.1     Würzburger Hofbräu, AG | over 50 |

Note: a. Also over 25 per cent owned by 1.
Source: Adapted from data in Commerzbank, *Wer gehört zu wem* (Düsseldorf, May 1982).

Bayerische Hypotheken- und Wechselbank and Dresdner Bank which jointly own over one half of the largest brewer (DUB Schultheiss), which in turn substantially owns 14 others. An idea of the complexity involved is revealed by Haake-Beck (4.1.1.1.1) which is over 75 per cent owned by Beck (4.1.1.1), which is majority-owned by Kaiser (4.1.1), which is a wholly owned subsidiary of Holsten (4.1). But Holsten is over 25 per cent owned by the Vereins- und Westbank (4). Added to this labyrinth is the fact that the latter bank is itself over 25 per cent owned by another bank, the Bayerische Vereinsbank (3).

In the case of Bayerische Hypotheken- und Wechselbank, the policy of holding equity in beer companies was an outgrowth of a managerial decision in the late 1960s to create a brewery empire. This policy included facilitating a merger between DUB and Schultheiss to set up the nation's largest brewer. Spurring bank ownership in the beer industry was the attraction that certain brewers are large owners of real estate, with Löwenbräu reported to be Munich's largest real estate owner. Among the other major TNBs with weighty equity commitments in alcohol TNCs are France's Paribas and Crédit Suisse, one of Switzerland's big three banks.[13]

Loans and credit lines are the second medium through which banks interact with the alcohol industry. As in most industries, the biggest TNCs can raise the largest loans on the most lucrative terms. Well could Seagram declare with respect to their $3 billion Euro-dollar loan that 'thirty-one banks participated, an unusually small number for such a large credit, and the time in which the financing was accomplished was unusually short'.[14] Likewise, banks are now playing a central role in pushing through and financing mergers and acquisitions. France's Banque de l'Union Européenne, to take but one example, has assumed a leading role in the recent spate of mergers among champagne producers. Such large-scale bank involvement is by no means confined to DME corporations, but is also discernible in large firms of certain developing economies.[15]

**In a Few Words**

This work was designed to provide an overview of the trajectory of alcoholic beverage sectors over the past two decades via three prisms: output, trade and consumption in the global market: corporate structures in production and distribution; and marketing strategies. It is through these prisms that the authors have analysed the increasing internationalisation of alcohol markets as well as rapidly changing patterns on national markets.

It is only through such a study of corporate structures and strategies that the basic conflict between the galaxy of institutions that dominate alcohol and public health can be understood. Likewise, other commodities which have a bearing on health, for example tobacco, pharmaceuticals, food and pesticides, are also increasingly dominated by TNCs, and call for analyses along similar lines.

As the current economic crisis deepens, the corporate institutions producing and marketing these products must become more concentrated, intensifying the conquest of national and international markets. This can only heighten the conflict between the ambitions of corporate power and public health.

# Notes

1. Arthur Burns, *The Decline of Competition: A Study of the Evolution of American Industry* (London, 1936), p. 76.
2. See Alfred Eichner, *The Megacorp and Oligopoly: Micro-Foundations and Macro-Dynamics* (Cambridge, 1976).
3. While Anheuser-Busch has been the traditional price leader in the US beer market, Philip Morris took over this role in the late 1970s, only to relinquish it back to Anheuser-Busch in the early 1980s. *Beverage World*, January 198▮.
4. Computed from prices in *Wine and Spirit*, May 1980.
5. *The Star* (Malaysia), 23 October 1980.
6. A variation on this strategy in periods of large-scale overcapacity involves creating 'cheap brands' for high quality beverages, which are sold on very slim margins to deplete stocks. Scotch whisky TNCs resorted to such brand techniques in large quantities in 1980 – 1. See *Wine and Spirit*, May 1981.
7. *Multinational Monitor*, December 1981.
8. Different cost structures for shirts made in the Republic of Korea and in the USA reveal the US retailer's scope for boosting profitability by utilising his own brand name on both shirts and selling them at the same price. Even with allowance made for transportation, tariff and quota charges to the USA, the cost differential would still be some 20 – 30 per cent. UNCTAD, *Fibres and Textiles*, p. 227.
9. This partially explains the hostility of certain French wine growers who dynamited 50,000 hectolitres of the Comptoir's stocks in March 1982. *Le Monde*, 13 March 1982.
10. *The Economist*, 1 November 1980.
11. Transfer pricing is also deployed to counter government price controls which prohibit retail margins that exceed a fixed percentage of the prices of imported goods or of production costs. To circumvent such regulatory measures, the alcoholic beverage TNCs can inflate costs of goods imported from their own subsidiary. Further, the transfer pricing mechanism has been used to switch profits and cash balances from countries with weak currencies to those with stronger currencies. To a no lesser extent, it has also been deployed to avoid foreign exchange controls. For a

fuller treatment of this subject, see Robin Murray (ed.), *Multinationals Beyond the Market: Intra-firm Trade and the Control of Transfer Pricing* (London, 1981).

12. Interlocking directorates between leading alcohol TNCs and TNBs are another, witnessed in Allied-Lyons ex-chairman, Sir Keith Showering, who was also a director of the Midland Bank. *Milling and Banking News*, 13 April 1982.

13. As of mid-1981, Paribas held 3 per cent of the equity of Carlton & United Breweries, Australia's largest brewer; 3 per cent of BSN Gervais Danone; and 4 per cent of the champagne house Heidsieck. Winefood, one of the largest groups in the Italian wine industry, came into Crédit Suisse's possession in 1977, when the bank took over the unauthorised investments of its Chiasso branch in a major banking scandal. *World Drinks Report*, 3 March 1981 and 21 July 1981.

14. Seagram, *Annual Report*, 1981.

15. Both large brewers in the Philippines found it relatively easy to negotiate multi-million dollar international syndicated loans in the early 1980s. *Brewing and Distilling International*, February 1980.

# INDEX

## 170 Index

Printed in the United States
by Baker & Taylor Publisher Services